To Be Or **Not To Be**

Shakespeare

NOW!

Series edited by: Simon Palfrey and Ewan Fernie

To Be Or **Not To Be**

Douglas Bruster

continuum

Continuum
The Tower Building
11 York Road
London
SE1 7NX
www.continuumbooks.com

80 Maiden Lane
Suite 704
New York
NY 10038

British Library Cataloguing-in-Publication Data
A catalogue record for this book is available from the British Library.

ISBN-10: HB: 0-8264-8997-4
       PB: 0-8264-8998-2
ISBN-13: HB: 9780826489975
       PB: 9780826489982

Library of Congress Cataloging-in-Publication Data
A catalog record for this book is available from the Library of Congress.

Typeset by BookEns Ltd, Royston, Herts.
Printed and bound by Athenaeum Press Ltd, Gateshead, Tyne and Wear

Contents

General Editors' Preface

Shakespeare Now! represents a new form for new approaches. Whereas academic writing is far too often ascendant and detached, attesting all too clearly to years of specialist training, *Shakespeare Now!* offers a series of intellectual adventure stories: animate with fresh and often exposed thinking, with ideas still heating in the mind.

This series of 'minigraphs' will thus help to bridge two yawning gaps in current public discourse. First, the gap between scholarly thinking and a public audience: the assumption of academics that they cannot speak to anyone but their peers unless they hopelessly dumb-down their work. Second, the gap between public audience and scholarly thinking: the assumption of regular playgoers, readers, or indeed actors that academics write about the plays at a level of abstraction or specialization that they cannot hope to understand.

But accessibility should not be mistaken for comfort or predictability. Impatience with scholarly obfuscation is usually accompanied by a basic impatience with anything but (supposed) common sense. What this effectively means is a distrust of really thinking, and a disdain for anything that might unsettle conventional assumptions, particularly through crossing or re-drafting formal, political, or theoretical boundaries. We encourage such adventure, and base our claim to a broad audience upon it.

Here, then, is where our series is innovative: no compromising of the sorts of things that can be thought; a commitment to publishing powerful cutting-edge scholarship; *but* a conviction that these things are essentially communicable, that we can find a language that is enterprising, individual, and shareable.

To achieve this we need a form that can capture the genuine challenge and vigour of thinking. Shakespeare is intellectually exciting, and so too are the ideas and debates that thinking about his work can provoke. But published scholarship often fails to communicate much of this. It is difficult to sustain excitement over the 80–120,000 words customary for a monograph: difficult enough for the writer, and perhaps even more so for the reader. Scholarly articles have likewise become a highly formalised mode not only of publication, but also of intellectual production. The brief length of articles means that a concept can be outlined, but its implications or application can rarely be tested in detail. The decline of sustained, exploratory attention to the singularity of a play's language, occasion, or movement is one of the unfortunate results. Often 'the play' is somehow assumed, a known and given thing that is not really worth exploring. So we spend our time pursuing collateral contexts: criticism becomes a belated, historicizing footnote.

Important things have got lost. Above all, any vivid sense as to why we are bothered with these things in the first place. Why read? Why go to plays? Why are they important? How does any pleasure they give relate to any of the things we labour to say about them? In many ways, literary criticism has forgotten affective and political immediacy. It has assumed a shared experience of the plays and then averted the gaze from any such experience, or any testing of it. We want a more ductile and sensitive mode of production; one that has more chance of capturing what people are really thinking and reading about, rather than what the pre-empting imperatives of journal or respectable monograph tend to encourage.

Furthermore, there is a vast world of intellectual possibility – from the past and the present – that mainstream Shakespeare criticism has all but ignored. In recent years there has been a move away from 'theory' in literary studies: an aversion to its obscure jargon and complacent self-regard; a sense that its tricks were too easily rehearsed and that the whole game has become one of diminishing returns. This has further encouraged a retreat into the supposed safety of historicism. Of course the best such work is stimulating, revelatory, and indispensable. But too often there is little trace of any struggle; little sense that the writer is coming at the subject afresh, searching for the most appropriate language or method. Alternatively, the prose is so labored that all trace of an urgent story is quite lost.

We want to open up the sorts of thinking – and thinkers – that might help us get at what Shakespeare is doing or why Shakespeare matters. This might include psychology, cognitive science, theology, linguistics, phenomenology, metaphysics, ecology, history, political theory; it can mean other art forms such as music, sculpture, painting, dance; it can mean the critical writing itself becomes a creative act.

In sum, we want the minigraphs to recover what the Renaissance 'essay' form was originally meant to embody. It meant an 'assay' – a trial or a test of something; putting something to the proof; and doing so in a form that is not closed-off and that cannot be reduced to a system. We want to communicate intellectual activity at its most alive: when it is still exciting to the one doing it; when it is questing and open, just as Shakespeare is. Literary criticism – that is, really thinking about words in action, plays as action – can start making a much more creative and vigorous contribution to contemporary intellectual *life*.

Simon Palfrey and Ewan Fernie

To be or not to be

To be, or not to be, that is the question: 55
Whether 'tis nobler in the mind to suffer
The slings and arrows of outrageous fortune,
Or to take arms against a sea of troubles,
And by opposing, end them. To die, to sleep –
No more, and by a sleep to say we end   60
The heart-ache and the thousand natural shocks
That flesh is heir to; 'tis a consummation
Devoutly to be wish'd. To die, to sleep –
To sleep, perchance to dream – ay, there's the rub,
For in that sleep of death what dreams may come,   65
When we have shuffled off this mortal coil,
Must give us pause; there's the respect
That makes calamity of so long life:
For who would bear the whips and scorns of time,
Th' oppressor's wrong, the proud man's contumely,   70
The pangs of despis'd love, the law's delay,
The insolence of office, and the spurns
That patient merit of th' unworthy takes,
When he himself might his quietus make
With a bare bodkin; who would fardels bear,   75
To grunt and sweat under a weary life,
But that the dread of something after death,
The undiscover'd country, from whose bourn
No traveller returns, puzzles the will,
And makes us rather bear those ills we have,   80
Than fly to others that we know not of?
Thus conscience does make cowards of us all,
And thus the native hue of resolution
Is sicklied o'er with the pale cast of thought,
And enterprises of great pitch and moment   85
With this regard their currents turn awry,
And lose the name of action. – Soft you now,
The fair Ophelia.

1 In the Shakespeare Museum

Imagine finding yourself in the Shakespeare Museum. You walk through its vast marble hallways, looking into entire rooms set aside for Shakespeare's plays, poems, and even characters. Here you find a gallery of artefacts from *A Midsummer Night's Dream* – among them editions, portraits and costumes. Across the hall an equally large *Macbeth* room presents the daggers, witches' cauldrons, and crowns used by hundreds of actors down through the centuries. Continuing on, you encounter a sizeable space for Juliet and Romeo, and then a separate gallery for the Sonnets. As you move from room to room, taking in these sights, you realize with some amusement that you have also been listening to Shakespeare's words. Everywhere snatches of songs and familiar speeches float through the air. In this hallway, Ariel sings *The Tempest*'s haunting melody, 'Full fadom five.' Around the corner you hear the stately cadence of 'Friends, Romans, countrymen' from *Julius Caesar*.

Just ahead, though, you catch sight of the most arresting thing of all. For here, off the Museum's expansive *Hamlet* wing, you come across an entire gallery devoted to the 'To be or not to be' speech. Walking past rows of skulls, rapiers, and portraits of Hamlets gone by, you step into this shadowy room set aside for Hamlet's famous soliloquy.

As you enter, the exhibit springs almost magically to life. From the darkness, the afternoon sun comes up on an Elizabethan production of the play. Standing near the front of a wide wooden platform, an actor in hose and doublet begins the famous soliloquy: *To be* . . . Before he can finish this line, another stage in a different part of the room is illuminated, this time by torches. You turn your head and see the same actor delivering the speech less broadly, his voice lowered for what appears to be a more intimate setting: *or not to be* . . . Both Hamlets speak at once, and are joined in quick order by a third figure: *that is the question.* Dressed less formally than the others, this Hamlet bobs up and down slightly as he gives his lines. You note with some surprise that he stands on the deck of an Elizabethan ship. More strange still, this ship – from what you can tell of the distant background – seems to be anchored off coastal Africa.

The words of this familiar speech unfold while your eyes and ears dart from Hamlet to Hamlet, taking in differences among their costumes, stages, and manner of delivery. When a fourth and fifth actor appear, you realize that you are seeing and hearing productions of *Hamlet* from Shakespeare's time forward. For a brief moment they continue the speech as a small group: *whether 'tis nobler in the mind* . . . And as you watch and listen to them you notice something interesting. Even as they deliver the lines to unseen audiences, many of these Hamlets peek at the actors who have come before them. Although they cannot avoid adding their own style to the performance, each tries to do what his predecessors have done.

The speech continues, and this room – which you now recognize is enormous – begins to fill up with more Hamlets and more stages. They appear in a faster tempo, and, as the decades pass, the differences among them increase. The stages, once thrust out into the crowd or even a part of the audience's own space, have been pulled back and crowned with high, arched fronts. In contrast to the sunlight shining on the first actor, candles – literally footlights – illuminate many of the dozens of Hamlets now speaking. Their costumes have changed as well. Unlike the hose and doublets of the first

Hamlets, the more recent actors wear coats and wigs of the eighteenth century. They still pay attention to those who have started before them, but instead of imitating their predecessors these actors strive to be slightly different. One speaks his lines in an easy, almost conversational way: *to suffer the slings and arrows of outrageous fortune* . . .

As the eighteenth century gives way to the nineteenth, the words of the soliloquy continue, but not as coherently as before. Most of the Hamlets perform in a more formal, declamatory style: *or by taking arms against a sea of troubles* . . . Your attention lingers on one of these Hamlets, for you note with interest a woman costumed as the Prince. She catches your eye as she says *and by opposing, end them*.

More Hamlets appear. Their costumes and the scenery they stand before vary from what has come earlier. Some stages present the battlements of a castle, others the interior of a medieval court. A few of these stages are cavernous, dwarfing their speakers. Still more come into view, and in ever quickening succession. The words of the soliloquy start to run together as you grow overwhelmed by the number of actors. A man speaking in Romanian joins the bevy of European performers reciting the speech in their own languages; he keeps pace with the French, German, Russian, Spanish, and Italian Hamlets already speaking.

Suddenly, in another corner of this room, a spotlight picks out a gramophone. Out of its horn-shaped speaker a scratchy, unreal voice joins the chorus: *To sleep, perchance to dream* . . . Behind this machine, others start into motion as if by magic. Their needles ride the grooves of thick black records rotating slowly atop turntables, adding more voices to the chorus you hear: *ay, there's the rub* . . .

Still other machines materialize as the twentieth century dawns. An illuminated screen begins to glow on one of the gallery's walls. Its images of a darkly garbed Hamlet pulse with the uneven rhythms of early film. You see his lips move in synch with the words of the speech, but you do not hear his voice. Instead, the sequence cuts to a subtitle. You read the words of the soliloquy in an elegant white font against a decorated black square: *For who would bear the whips and scorns of time . . .?*

Before you can finish reading even a few words though, a radio crackles to life in the foreground, its ghostly broadcast of Hamlet's words joining the hundreds already audible. Other screens continue to flicker on, drawing your attention. The first glow silently with subtitles, but soon others burst into life with the sounds of recorded speech. You recognize a few of these voices and faces, marveling not only at how young these actors looked in their prime, but also at the fact that the Hamlets themselves have become younger. The men and women you have encountered so far have tended to be middle-aged and older. These modern Hamlets are in their thirties, even twenties.

The sheer number of Hamlets performing all around you makes things almost too much to process. Even as new machines join the chorus, stages continue to pop up, some quite barren, some decorated very imaginatively. Screen after screen cascades into life, and soon the walls of the gallery are filled with hundreds of different Hamlets delivering their lines: *the undiscover'd country . . .* If the earlier actors had glanced at their counterparts while speaking, these latest Hamlets strike you as looking almost wildly around them. Like you, they seem intimidated by the number of speakers who have come before. Their response is fairly uniform. These Hamlets struggle to be different. Some speak directly to the audience; one to Ophelia. They change their gestures and the cadences of their lines, delivering them in slightly improbable postures as though trying to prevent you from imitating them or predicting their action.

Even the relationship of actor to speech changes now. Where the Hamlets of early film had moved their lips silently to the speech, one of the more recent screen-Hamlets seems to 'think' it. His lips do not move, but some of the words are audible as an interior monologue. You watch in amazement as the four walls of this room throb with light: *the pale cast of thought* ... Many dozens of screen and television-Hamlets add their versions to the choir already speaking.

Finally, startlingly, the speech comes to an end – *Soft you now, the fair Ophelia*. Like a wind-up toy, the soliloquy eases to a halt. The stages and screens go dark as silence fills the room again, which now feels empty and cold. You are left alone with your thoughts. As you turn to leave, a small plaque near the door catches your eye. It describes the speech in the compressed language of museum exhibits everywhere:

'To be or not to be'

This soliloquy by Prince Hamlet stands as one of Shakespeare's most celebrated speeches. From the time it was first heard on Elizabethan stages, it has been imitated, translated, venerated, and parodied. In the process, it has become a symbol for theatricality, the Shakespearean, philosophy, and even literature itself. The speech has been set to music many times, and each of its phrases has been borrowed for the title of a subsequent creative work. Hamlet's speech is recited on stage and in classrooms worldwide on a daily basis. Actors and audiences alike recognize it as a masterpiece of dramatic writing.

To be or not to be

To be, or not to be, that is the question: 55
Whether 'tis nobler in the mind to suffer
The slings and arrows of outrageous fortune,
Or to take arms against a sea of troubles,
And by opposing, end them. To die, to sleep –
No more, and by a sleep to say we end   60
The heart-ache and the thousand natural shocks
That flesh is heir to; 'tis a consummation
Devoutly to be wish'd. To die, to sleep –
To sleep, perchance to dream – ay, there's the rub,
For in that sleep of death what dreams may come,   65
When we have shuffled off this mortal coil,
Must give us pause; there's the respect
That makes calamity of so long life:
For who would bear the whips and scorns of time,
Th' oppressor's wrong, the proud man's contumely,   70
The pangs of despis'd love, the law's delay,
The insolence of office, and the spurns
That patient merit of th' unworthy takes,
When he himself might his quietus make
With a bare bodkin; who would fardels bear,   75
To grunt and sweat under a weary life,
But that the dread of something after death,
The undiscover'd country, from whose bourn
No traveller returns, puzzles the will,
And makes us rather bear those ills we have,   80
Than fly to others that we know not of?
Thus conscience does make cowards of us all,
And thus the native hue of resolution
Is sicklied o'er with the pale cast of thought,
And enterprises of great pitch and moment   85
With this regard their currents turn awry,
And lose the name of action. – Soft you now,
The fair Ophelia.

2 What are the Questions?

If there *were* a Shakespeare Museum like the one described here, it would definitely have some kind of *Hamlet* wing, so central is this play to Shakespeare's achievement. And this *Hamlet* wing would in turn be likely to reserve a great deal of space for the 'To be or not to be' soliloquy. We have imagined a special room in which all the performances of this speech down through history were played in overlapping sequence. This cumulative staging is one way of coming to grips with a speech that lies at the heart of Shakespeare's most revered play. *Hamlet* was most likely a triumph for Shakespeare as a playwright, and its subsequent success has made it a metaphor for his larger achievements. As delivered by such star performers as Richard Burbage, David Garrick, Sarah Bernhardt, John Barrymore, Laurence Olivier, and Kenneth Branagh, this speech has proven integral to the public's image of Shakespeare.

It is not too much of an exaggeration to say that the speech has helped shape the way the theater, acting, and even thinking itself have been conceived in the West. Indeed, while the 'To be or not to be' soliloquy works as a metaphor for both the play and the playwright, it also stands in for a certain version of his culture. We could recall, for instance, that *Hamlet* was performed aboard the Elizabethan ship named the Red Dragon off the coast of Sierra Leone in 1607 – perhaps the first time the play was staged outside England. To keep in mind a mental picture of that gently rolling deck so far from home may help us imagine the larger stage of Western culture, and

Shakespeare's place on it. His stand-in on this crowded platform is Hamlet, both play and Prince. Like an Elizabethan ship hundreds of miles from home, Shakespeare's words have traversed the world. And if Hamlet has been a central emissary of that journey, the 'To be or not to be' soliloquy has become a version-in-miniature of this most celebrated writer's most celebrated play and character.

Even in its flattering description of the speech's monumental nature, though, the tidy version of this soliloquy that we have read in our museum's placard tells only half the story. For instance, if the speech is a 'masterpiece' – which suggests a work to which the artist has applied finishing touches – why have actors had to work so hard to find meaning in it? We could consider the odd fact that the more Hamlets there were in our museum scenario, the less comfortable they seemed to be with the speech. The most recent Hamlets, in particular, seemed to carry upon their backs the burden of all the earlier performances. 'How can I make it new?' each seemed to ask. 'How am I to deliver the speech, when it has been delivered so many thousands of times before?'

They would have a point in asking 'How can I say these words at all?' While Hamlet's 'To be or not to be' soliloquy remains one of the central speeches in all of Western culture, it is also one of the most mysterious. There are reasons for this mystery. Unlike the description on our placard, the speech as a whole is actually quite messy. And its beginning (the most orderly part of the soliloquy) seems so familiar that we think we know the entire speech better than we do. No matter how many times we hear it begun, though, it is easy for us to get lost in its middle and end. The disorder of this speech, in fact, can produce a kind of trance in its readers and hearers. As we will see, the speech turns on itself time and again, sometimes like the back-and-forth rallies in a tennis match, at others like the coils of a snake moving sideways through the grass.

It is important to realize straightaway that the overwhelming question usually asked of this speech – 'Is it about suicide?' – is hardly the most interesting thing it asks us to ask. In fact, one could say that the speech does not ask us to think much about suicide at all. There is suicide *in* the speech, clearly, but Hamlet is interested in so many other things, and interested in them so profoundly, that calling 'To be or not to be' a suicide speech is to miss the point. It is to dwell on the pedestal of an imposing monument in order to avoid the vertigo that comes from looking up at its heights.

Other puzzles seem more pressing. Among these:

Why have so many actors sought to play Hamlet, only to struggle with this speech?

How could the most famous speech in literature be so mysterious, and so poorly understood?

But these are only a few of the uncertainties we may have. The soliloquy produces some troubling contradictions, things that don't seem to fit. We could phrase these as follows:

Why has this extremely public document come to serve as our most important declaration of the private?

Why has this account of the failures of the self become a verbal shrine to self-consciousness?

And, finally, perhaps the most troubling of all:

What does it mean that the central speech of the central character in the central play of the language's central author is all but useless to its speaker and story?

Even a much longer book on the 'To be or not to be' soliloquy would probably be unable to answer these questions with any finality. This is the nature of literature generally, and perhaps of *Hamlet* in particular. Where it *is* able to provide answers, this short book gives mainly provisional ones. But it does seek to discover and share some ways of wrestling with such questions. It attempts to do so by looking carefully at the speech from a number of angles. We will begin with what the soliloquy may mean.

To be or not to be

To be, or not to be, that is the question: 55
Whether 'tis nobler in the mind to suffer
The slings and arrows of outrageous fortune,
Or to take arms against a sea of troubles,
And by opposing, end them. To die, to sleep –
No more, and by a sleep to say we end   60
The heart-ache and the thousand natural shocks
That flesh is heir to; 'tis a consummation
Devoutly to be wish'd. To die, to sleep –
To sleep, perchance to dream – ay, there's the rub,
For in that sleep of death what dreams may come,   65
When we have shuffled off this mortal coil,
Must give us pause; there's the respect
That makes calamity of so long life:
For who would bear the whips and scorns of time,
Th' oppressor's wrong, the proud man's contumely,   70
The pangs of despis'd love, the law's delay,
The insolence of office, and the spurns
That patient merit of th' unworthy takes,
When he himself might his quietus make
With a bare bodkin; who would fardels bear,   75
To grunt and sweat under a weary life,
But that the dread of something after death,
The undiscover'd country, from whose bourn
No traveller returns, puzzles the will,
And makes us rather bear those ills we have,   80
Than fly to others that we know not of?
Thus conscience does make cowards of us all,
And thus the native hue of resolution
Is sicklied o'er with the pale cast of thought,
And enterprises of great pitch and moment   85
With this regard their currents turn awry,
And lose the name of action. – Soft you now,
The fair Ophelia.

3 There's the Rub

What does the 'To be or not to be' soliloquy mean? Eventually we will ask this question in other ways. We will pay special attention to *how* this speech means (its style, structure, and rhythms), *where* it does so (in a story and often on a stage), and for *whom* (Hamlet, among others). Ideally, we could look at all these things at once. And in reality, the *how*, *where*, and *for whom* all have an important role in the *what* of the speech's meaning. To separate these things is to postpone issues that can help us toward deeper understanding. But obviously the soliloquy is complicated. And taking its various aspects and contexts one by one seems a good way to address its complexities. This focused approach is particularly helpful in relation to the interpretation of the speech that one hears so often: that it is a 'suicide speech.' There *are* suicide speeches in Shakespeare, and perhaps even in *Hamlet*, but this is not one of them. We will see, in fact, that this speech runs counter to the clichéd reading. Let us look at it and listen to it closely, rewinding it (only to play it again) in the pages that follow.

Our main version of the speech comes from *The Riverside Shakespeare*, 2nd edition. All the Shakespeare citations in this book refer to this edition. For the record, the *Riverside* bases its text of *Hamlet* primarily on the second Quarto (abbreviated as 'Q2'), originally published in 1604/5. Three versions of this speech survive from Shakespeare's time. Two – that from Q2 and the First Folio ('F1,' published 1623) – are almost exactly the same. Another version of *Hamlet* – probably a kind of 'bootleg' edition – was printed in 1603;

this is called the 'bad quarto' or, less prejudicially, the 'first quarto' (Q1). We will look at its less familiar version of this speech later in this book. For now, it is enough to observe that in standard editions the speech itself occurs approximately 60 lines into the first scene of Act 3; in our text, it is printed at lines 55 through 89. To make the following analysis easier to read, subsequent quotations from the soliloquy will be bolded, and the blank verse's capital letters will be retained only if they begin a sentence – thus **Whether 'tis nobler** becomes **whether 'tis nobler**. Clearly, suppressing the capitalization, like losing the line breaks themselves, lends ease to the reading process at the expense of the verse lines. It is a calculated trade-off. Finally, you may notice that while the text here (like most modern editions) features a comma after '**To be**,' this book follows conventional practice in referring to the 'To be or not to be' soliloquy. Here is the speech itself:

To be, or not to be, that is the question: 55
Whether 'tis nobler in the mind to suffer
The slings and arrows of outrageous fortune,
Or to take arms against a sea of troubles,
And by opposing, end them. To die, to sleep—
No more, and by a sleep to say we end   60
The heart-ache and the thousand natural shocks
That flesh is heir to; 'tis a consummation
Devoutly to be wish'd. To die, to sleep—
To sleep, perchance to dream—ay, there's the rub,
For in that sleep of death what dreams may come,   65
When we have shuffled off this mortal coil,
Must give us pause; there's the respect
That makes calamity of so long life:
For who would bear the whips and scorns of time,
Th' oppressor's wrong, the proud man's contumely,   70
The pangs of despis'd love, the law's delay,

The insolence of office, and the spurns
That patient merit of th' unworthy takes,
When he himself might his quietus make
With a bare bodkin; who would fardels bear,   75
To grunt and sweat under a weary life,
But that the dread of something after death,
The undiscover'd country, from whose bourn
No traveller returns, puzzles the will,
And makes us rather bear those ills we have,   80
Than fly to others that we know not of?
Thus conscience does make cowards of us all,
And thus the native hue of resolution
Is sicklied o'er with the pale cast of thought,
And enterprises of great pitch and moment   85
With this regard their currents turn awry,
And lose the name of action.——Soft you now,
The fair Ophelia.

The architecture of the speech will concern us more in the next chapter of this book. But noticing a deep symmetry may immediately shed some light on the first line's power. Hamlet's first line – perhaps the most famous in all of literature – breaks in half, and each of its halves breaks in half again:

1				2		
To be,	*or*	**not to be**		**that**	*is the*	**question**
1		2		1		2

The line's familiarity may derive in part from its perfectly symmetrical nature. Its balanced halves (**To be, or not to be, / that is the question**) themselves balance atop a middle word (**or**) or words (**is the**). Another structure comes into play as well. Like the total in a mathematical equation (2 + 2 = 4) or the reckoning in a shop's tally sheet (5p + 5p = 10p), the last word sums up the line's first half.

But what is a **question**? This word meant something particular in Shakespeare's time. It referred to a formal issue for meditation or debate. Students at university or law school in the Elizabethan era, for instance, would typically be required to argue an announced **question**. These 'questions' ranged from the practical – such as 'whether a man should marry' – to the more speculative – for instance, 'whether there be more worlds than this one.' As it does in *Hamlet*, the form of the **question** trickled into many Elizabethan writings. One finds a contemporary author wondering, for example, whether poetry or philosophy has more force in teaching. In another text, a character asks whether it is better (on one hand) to revel in one's youth and later regret one's sins or (on the other hand) to postpone the enjoyment of pleasure. Clearly these 'questions' balance alternatives, and ask that we consider each point of view. The alternatives of such 'questions' mean our line's items diverge as well as combine. Thus not only 2 + 2 = 4 but 2, −2 = ?

Surprisingly, the speech begins to get complicated with the apparently simple word **that**. For this word does two things at once, and neither of these things makes matters clearer. First, it prevents the line from gaining clarity – the kind of clarity that could result, for instance, had Shakespeare finished the line with something like 'To be or not to be melancholy is . . .' That is, had he completed the line not with a characterization (**that**), but by making clear what **To be** and **not to be** mean. Second, it misleads us by implying that what comes before it (**To be, or not to be**) has the clarity it does not provide.

The first half of this line *is* a question. It is a question, though, not only in the sense of an academic alternative, but also in posing a puzzle that asks to be solved. What does Hamlet suggest when he sets out the alternative of **To be, or not to be**?

By **to be**, Hamlet could mean (among other things) 'to live' or 'to exist,' with **not to be** thus implying 'to die' or 'to cease to exist.' It is important to note that the division here – being and not being – was one of the stable alternatives in philosophy at the time. Doctor Faustus, the cerebral title character of Christopher Marlowe's great tragedy (written about a decade before *Hamlet*), actually takes up this **question** in its Greek form – *on kai me on* ('being and not being' – pronounced 'own kai may own'). Faustus attributes this issue to Aristotle, and discards it as not pragmatic enough for his tastes. In this philosophical register, **To be, or not to be** provides a mutually incompatible contradiction; things have to be one way or the other: either they exist or they do not. A contemporary form of Hamlet's proposition in Latin reads *est aut non est*: that is, the question of whether something 'is or is not.'

So far so good. But this apparently straightforward choice needs to be qualified with other possibilities. This is especially the case because the speech's next lines include yet another alternative. It may be helpful to represent this alternative by means of a diagram. Here the well-known **whether** clause supports a balanced set of choices:

whether 'tis nobler

in the mind to suffer		**to take arms against a**
the slings and arrows	**or**	**sea of troubles and by**
of outrageous fortune		**opposing, end them.**

These lines pose alternatives by means of memorable imagery. At base, the choice is between stoicism (the commitment to accepting what life brings one – whether good or ill – with equal indifference) and heroism (the act of doing something decisive by means of personal force – the very opposite of indifference). The **whether** here, like the **that** of the preceding line, implies that a problem is being solved through definition. But this definition actually does the opposite. Seemingly clarifying the alternative of **To be, or not to be**, it multiplies possibilities rather than subtracting them. This multiplication of possibilities comes from the ambiguities of words (what

being and **not be**ing mean, for instance) and reference (which of these alternatives is being referred to by the **whether** definitions).

In addition to our 'life or death' reading, **To be** could mean something like 'to act' and **not to be**, 'not to act.' This would connect **To be** with **to take arms** and **not to be** with **suffer**. Thus **To be** could imply the heroic possibility mentioned in the following lines and **not to be** the stoic possibility. But − and this is crucial to note − the phrase **To be** could also embrace the stoic possibility, in the sense that Hamlet may mean the acceptance of *not acting* (against, say, the King). This reading is especially relevant to the topic of suicide that comes up later in the speech with the phrase **his quietus make with a bare bodkin**: not only because inaction seems the opposite of suicide, but because the result in each case may be the same. A **bodkin** is a short, pointed weapon such as a dagger; it is **bare** because it has been drawn from its sheath in order to be used.

By this point in the play, Hamlet has been confronted with a number of challenges. The most important question he faces is whether he should act against the King (Claudius) as the Ghost has instructed him. However ambiguous those orders may be, the plea to 'revenge' his father's murder is urgent, as well as perilous. Hamlet is initially alone among the living in suspecting that his uncle has murdered his, Hamlet's, father − the lawful monarch of Denmark. As Hamlet discovers, gaining revenge will mean at the very least putting his life on the line, and possibly sacrificing it. His accidental, careless taking of Polonius' life, for example, helps set in motion the forces that will end his own.

To this dangerous action against the King, we may wish to add the possibility of Hamlet acting in another way − against himself. Whether intended, the mention of suicide later in his speech has led many to interpret his initial alternatives in that light as well. This multiplies the kinds of things that his opening words can mean but it does not change the basic possibilities. These possibilities, as we have seen, are generated in part from the verbal ambiguity (what **be**ing and

not being mean) and in part from which of these terms pairs, respectively, with the stoic (**in the mind to suffer**) and heroic (**to take arms**) explanations.

Here are some of the possibilities set out in a chart, with the subcategories represented in their own complexity:

To be		**not to be**	
1a	live/exist	1b	die/cease to exist
	(heroic)		*(stoic)*
2a	act (against King)	2b	not act (against King)
2a^1	act (against self)	2b^1	not act (against self)
	(stoic)		*(heroic)*
3a	accept not acting (against King)	3b	refuse inaction (against King)
3a^1	accept not acting (against self)	3b^1	refuse inaction (against self)

The middle rows above ('act/not act') show us that, depending on how we translate his words, Hamlet's heroism may lead to death (**not to be**) as well as life (**To be**), and that stoicism may likewise lead to his death (**not to be**) or allow him to live (**To be**). That is, we recognize here that each of our terms (**To be** and **not to be**) can be read to imply one thing *and its exact opposite*. The paradox is that the middle categories (2a and 2b) contradict those that sandwich them. Thus a 'heroic' reading of **To be** (2a and 2a^1) gives us a Hamlet who will die (that is, 1b, our first-level interpretation of **not ... be**) through his murderous action against the King (revenge – which may lead to his own death) or himself (suicide). Likewise a stoic **not to be** (2b and 2b^1) gives us a Hamlet who may live (1a, our first-level reading of **To be**) through not acting against either himself (suicide) or the King (revenge).

Here is the same chart with the contradiction represented by means of arrows:

To be		**not to be**	
1a	live/exist	1b	die/cease to exist
	(*heroic*)		(*stoic*)
2a	act (against King)	2b	not act (against King)
$2a^1$	act (against self)	$2b^1$	not act (against self)
	(stoic)		(*heroic*)
3a	accept not acting (against King)	3b	refuse inaction (against King)
$3a^1$	accept not acting (against self)	$3b^1$	refuse inaction (against self)

It is vital to recognize this contradiction because the 'To be or not to be' soliloquy exposes us to this kind of puzzling logic at several other key moments. We can see it at work, for instance, in the very next stage of the speech.

Hamlet builds on the word **end** in the phrase **and by opposing, end them**. At this point he says **to die, to sleep – no more . . .** In both the second quarto (Q2) and Folio version, this line is given without punctuation as **to die to sleep no more**. One reading of **no more** sees Hamlet as summarizing the state he has earlier set out as **not to be** (as in, 'I would *be no more*'). In part because Hamlet will go on to envision death as a kind of **sleep**, many editions of the play, including the *Riverside* from which we have drawn our text, represent the phrase **no more** as Hamlet interrupting himself. Perhaps he may be talking to himself like a writer or rehearsing speaker. Like all of us, such figures may chide themselves for starting down a path without being ready to do so. Hamlet interrupts himself in this manner when reciting a passage from the Player's speech earlier in the play:

If it live in your memory, begin at this line – let me see, let me see:

The rugged Pyrrhus, like th' Hyrcanian beast –
'Tis not so, it begins with Pyrrhus:
The rugged Pyrrhus, he whose sable arms . . .

(2.2.448–52)

This seems precisely the kind of false start that Hamlet gives us with **no more**. He may step outside himself as if to admonish himself or drive a thought out of his head. This emphasis on his thoughts comes out, of course, in the puzzling phrase **nobler in the mind to suffer**: we can take this to mean 'suffering X seems nobler in one's mind,' or 'suffering in one's mind (rather than externally) seems nobler.' In part because Hamlet speaks to and with himself, his meaning remains ambiguous.

Hamlet imagines death as a kind of **sleep**. This sleep, again, restates the **'end'** of **by opposing, end them**. He makes the analogy pointedly with the phrase **by a sleep to *say* we**, just as we could say, for instance, 'by X here I mean Y.' As we have seen, the speech begins with careful if complicated alternatives, visible in the first line's pivotal **or** and expanded by the subsequent **whether** clause. But this has now given way to extensive restatement. Where the first line restated its alternatives as a single **question**, the next section of the speech restates again and again, as though Hamlet is dissatisfied with the initial results. Taking up the **end** that comes from **opposing a sea of troubles**, he asks us to imagine, with him, a **sleep** that will **end the heart-ache** and **thousand natural shocks that flesh is heir to**. His mode of restatement continues when **heart-ache** and **natural shocks** pick up the **slings and arrows of outrageous fortune**. Even as **fortune** inevitably throws hardships at our persons (the metaphor of **slings and arrows** is a powerful one here), so does being in a body make one **heir to** spiritual and physical troubles. The **heart-ache** and **shocks** may function as the imagined result of the **slings and arrows**.

Hamlet appears to conclude his line of thinking in the same way he ends his first line, with a summation of sorts: **'tis a consummation devoutly to be wish'd**. This resembles and echoes **that is the question** but shifts from an academic register (raised by the debate-word **question**) to a religious one with the words **consummation** and **devoutly**. Hamlet means something like 'this is a goal worth wishing for.' Separately, **consummation** and **devoutly** could be read without reference to religion. But together (and we will notice that Hamlet pairs them in his sentence), they invite us to consider the subject of death (**To die, to sleep**) in a religious context. The word **consummation** recalls the Latin form of Christ's last words on the cross: *'Consummatum est,'* or 'It is finished.' We can sense the power this phrase had for the Elizabethans in the fact that Marlowe has his eponymous character blasphemously parody them in *Doctor Faustus*, as he finishes signing a contract with Satan. By itself, the word **devoutly** would not necessarily invoke a religious context. In the immediate company of **consummation** here, however, it suggests **to be wish'd** may be a form of prayer, translated from a sacred to a secular domain.

At this point, the soliloquy appears to have settled its thoughts about the **sleep of death**. Hamlet has for a few lines taken up the metaphor of **death** as a kind of **sleep**, and has further entertained the notion that such a **sleep** would **end** the **troubles** of life. He has expressed these **troubles** as **heart-ache** and **the thousand natural shocks that flesh is heir to**. But having closed that line of thought by characterizing it as a secular prayer, something **devoutly to be wish'd**, he returns to it once more. The implication is that he is not satisfied with such an easy conclusion. Perhaps this lack of satisfaction centers on the word **wish'd**, for this can be taken in at least two ways. First, with its attendant words **to be**, it can suggest that such a **consummation** *should* be desired because it is a very desirable **end**. The phrase **to be wish'd** would thus have the force of something that needs to be done, in our sense of an item on a 'to do' list. But this word and phrase could also suggest that such an **end** must remain *only* a desire because it is ultimately too good to be true.

Hamlet will go on in the next section of the soliloquy to give us reasons this may be so. First, though, we could notice that he begins all over again with the same words he has used before: **To die, to sleep–. Where he had earlier settled on no more** as a stopping point, going on to imagine that **To die** is to experience an untroubled **sleep**, here he takes up **sleep** as a state of existence that shares with life the possibility of **heart-ache** and **natural shocks**. This trouble may come through **dreams**. Instead of imagining **sleep** as putting an **end** to such **troubles** (as he has done through his self-conscious definition, **and by a sleep to say we end . . .**), Hamlet repeats his initial metaphor (**death** as a kind of **sleep**) and follows out its implications. 'If we say that **death** is like **sleep**,' we can imagine him thinking, 'should we not be honest and admit that, just as when we slumber while alive, the **sleep of death** may bring dreams?' However seriously, Hamlet has already told Rosencrantz and Guildenstern that he could be content in life 'were it not that I have bad dreams' (2.2.254–6). Dreams were, for Shakespeare, a powerful, even central part of life. A later reader of Shakespeare's works, Sigmund Freud, saw dreams as one of the proofs that we have an unconscious, a faculty which steers us in ways we cannot, by definition, imagine. Unpredictable, dreams can terrify as well as soothe us with images over which we have no control. To be in the grips of a nightmare, as everyone knows, is to be absolutely helpless.

Thus when Hamlet begins his meditation over again, he re-defines **sleep** as an activity and experience rather than an **end**: **To die, to sleep – to sleep, perchance to dream . . .** Just as we have heard him talk to himself almost from outside himself in the 'Pyrrhus' rehearsal – 'let me see, let me see' – Hamlet stops momentarily to assure himself (as well as us) that he is now on a more fruitful track: **ay, there's the rub**.

This phrase has become so much a part of our language that we can misunderstand its meaning in this context. The term **rub** comes from the sport of bowling, where it was an obstacle to the bowler. Sometimes we use this phrase, **there's the rub**, as though it means merely 'there's the point.' We are perhaps tempted to do so by its echo of **that is the question**, but it means something different. In fact, we lose much of its significance if we take **rub** to mean merely 'point' or 'matter.' Calling upon its sense of 'obstacle' or 'impediment' – a simpler synonym would be 'block' – Hamlet lets us know that he has discovered something troubling. The possibility that the **sleep of death** may lead one to **dream** unsettles his first fantasy of death ending life's troubles. Revisiting his earlier analogy (where **death** is an untroubled **sleep**), Hamlet finds its blind spot, the **rub** that stands in the way.

The problem, Hamlet realizes, is that we **dream**. The end of life should not be imagined as the end of troubles, for even as our **flesh is heir to a thousand natural shocks**, so is our **sleep** not within our control. The next step in his soliloquy renders this fear apparent: **for in that sleep of death what dreams may come...** He makes the metaphor explicit: the **sleep of death**. Just as the word **that** worked to bring ambiguity to the soliloquy's first line, the word **what** (in **what dreams may come**) produces remarkable uncertainty. There are at least four things we could imagine arising from it; four ways that its sentence could end.

First, we could be tempted to read and hear it as signaling a question, as in 'For in that sleep of death what should one do if. . .?' The word **dreams** immediately following it closes down that possibility, of course, but leaves others open. For instance, the word **what** may lead us to imagine a question about the *kind* of dreams that could arise, as in 'What dreams come to us? True ones? False ones? Terrifying ones? Pleasing ones?' This second possibility finds itself joined by a third reading, in which the word **what** is an intensifier, as in 'What bad dreams I just had!' These latter readings remain in play until the word **must** two lines later, when we realize that Hamlet has another, fourth meaning in mind: **what dreams may come, when we have shuffled off this mortal coil, must give us pause**. He makes a declaration rather than asking a question. We could paraphrase it loosely as 'we have to consider seriously the possibility of dreaming after death.' Thus **what dreams** means something like *'the fact that* dreams [may come]' in addition, perhaps, to the second reading suggested above, the one involving the *kind* of dreams that may come. But it does not mean either of these things, we have noticed, until the sentence nears its end.

Hamlet means no more and no less than 'died' with the rich and poetic phrase **shuffled off this mortal coil**. But, like **there's the rub**, this phrase has become so much a part of our language that we have to work to hear its original contexts. These contexts are by no means simple. The phrase **shuffled off**, in fact, remains one of the most puzzling in the soliloquy. We share with the Elizabethans several senses of 'shuffle.' Like them, we 'shuffle' cards (a transitive use of 'shuffle'), and when we move our feet quickly along the ground we also speak of 'shuffling' them (an intransitive form of the verb). Which of these does Hamlet mean? We could start by noticing what they have in common: both of these actions involve a quick alternation of things (feet, cards).

To these senses, we could add another that Shakespeare uses in *Twelfth Night* when Sebastian complains about 'good turns' that 'Are shuffled off with such uncurrent pay' (3.3.15–16). Because 'uncurrent pay' means coins that are no longer valuable, Sebastian seems to be describing good deeds that are rewarded with underhanded ('shuffled off') trickery. Perhaps the act of shuffling cards – a moment where trickery has often transpired – influenced this sense of the verb, by which one could 'shuffle off' as a form of deception. Today we might say 'fob off,' 'pass off,' or even 'palm off' to convey this (Shakespeare used a form of 'fob off' in several of his plays). Sebastian's 'shuffled off ' may be linked to card-playing by these activities' basis in manual trickery: one gives someone false currency and false cards *by hand*, in close proximity.

Should we take **shuffled off** to be something done with the hands (the transitive sense) or the feet (intransitive)? Both senses seem to be present, especially when we compare uses of the word in contemporary texts. An anonymous play written about two decades after *Hamlet*, for instance, has a stage direction in which a character 'shuffles in.' Yet a pamphlet from roughly ten years prior to Shakespeare's play (a pamphlet famous for its early, mocking mention of the playwright) has a character promise to 'shuffle out' two unsavory figures for consideration. In this latter instance, we would say something like 'display' or 'parade before,' though the Elizabethan sense of having two misfits step humbly out is perfectly clear. In *The Merry Wives of Windsor* (written, like *Twelfth Night*, at about the time he wrote *Hamlet*), Shakespeare has Fenton remark that Ann Page's mother so favors another of her daughter's suitors that she has 'appointed' this suitor to 'shuffle her away, / While other sports are tasking of their minds' (4.6.28–30). Fenton's word picture, like the stage business that follows in his play, asks us to envision characters in disguise hurrying here and there around Windsor. This and other uses we have seen suggest that, with **shuffled off this mortal coil**, Hamlet may want us to imagine *both* someone stepping off the face of the earth – whether alternating their feet quickly, on purpose, or dragging them reluctantly – *and* someone getting rid of or otherwise dispensing of **this mortal coil**.

Shakespeare typically uses **coil** to refer to fuss and busy trouble, as when Ariel describes the confusion he has caused aboard ship in *The Tempest*, and Prospero responds 'My brave spirit! / Who was so firm, so constant, that this coil / Would not infect his reason?' (1.2.206–8). Shakespeare has Hamlet add **mortal** to the mix, extending the chaos of **coil** to the whole of our existence. The phrase **this mortal coil**, then, could be paraphrased as 'this troubling planet' or 'this turbulent life.'

And Sebastian's 'shuffle off' gives us another sense to consider, a sense in which **shuffled off** means something like 'deceived through a simple trick.' The trick here would be dying. In what way could dying prove deceptive? If we take Hamlet's cue and see **death** as a kind of **sleep**, perhaps by dying we 'trick' the world into believing that we are merely sleeping. In so doing, we have **shuffled off** the hubbub of our **mortal coil** with the false appearance of temporary (rather than permanent) rest. In this reading, while **mortal coil** refers primarily to 'human strife (or trouble),' there may be in **coil** a suggestion of ropes, which can **coil** around what they hold. Hamlet could be imagining life as a kind of bondage not only to be stepped away from, but to be wriggled out of by the trick of the **sleep of death**. If **coil** does succeed in asking us to imagine this, it adds to Hamlet's analogies. Where **death** is like **sleep**, **life** (a word he will use for the first time two lines later) is like being tied up in a **coil** that must eventually be **shuffled off**.

We can take Hamlet's **must give us pause** as meaning 'makes us stop,' or 'leads us to halt to consider.' The possibility that we **dream** after **death** leaves his first **consummation** as something that can only be **wish'd**. The **pause** comes from, and will explain, the **rub**. Even as he has carefully summarized various of his points already, Hamlet stops to explain the problem of **dreams** in the **sleep of death**: **there's the respect that makes calamity of so long life**. By **respect** here Hamlet seems to mean 'circumstances,' 'regard', or, less elegantly, 'the fact in relation to which.' His meaning may ask us to recognize the word's roots in Latin *re + spectare* (to look back at, regard, consider). We would perhaps say *per*spective or *re*gard rather than **respect**. Like **question** in the first line, **respect** has a formal, even academic ring to it. But it may also carry our more general sense of **respect** as something *to be* respected. Hamlet's choice of words may thus imply that **what dreams may come** in the **sleep of death** should be – may have to be – respected. We **respect** something we fear, and, as we have seen, nightmares are among the most frightening of **natural shocks**.

Mentioning **life** for the first time in this next line, Hamlet does so in a negative context. Echoing the first, 'm . . . k' sounds of **mortal coil**, he tells us that **respect** we have (whether as perspective or fear) for what may come after death **m**akes *c*alamity of life. The phrase **of so long life** may mean, literally, something like 'of life, which seems long.' But it suggests as well that having more time on earth means having more troubles, that **life** may be *too* **long**.

Hamlet's first line ends with a colon in the Folio version of his speech. As we saw, the **whether** clause appeared to explain (or to try to explain) that line's meaning. In the same way, both the Q2 and Folio versions of the speech have a colon following **calamity of so long life:**. This can tell the reader, actor and – through the actor – audience that what follows may explain or amplify his **respect** clause. Like **that is the question**, the phrase **there's the respect** both points back at what has come before and looks forward to something that comes after; as Hamlet puts it in a later soliloquy: 'such large discourse, / Looking before and after' (4.4.36–7).

What comes after **there's the respect** is a 13-line rhetorical question. We have two questions really, compounded in a long chain of negative instances:

Question no. 1:

> For who would bear the whips and scorns of time,
> Th' oppressor's wrong, the proud man's contumely,
> The pangs of despis'd love, the law's delay,
> The insolence of office, and the spurns
> That patient merit of th' unworthy takes,
> When he himself might his quietus make
> With a bare bodkin;

Question no. 2:

> who would fardels bear,
> To grunt and sweat under a weary life,
> But that the dread of something after death,
> The undiscover'd country, from whose bourn
> No traveller returns, puzzles the will,
> And makes us rather bear those ills we have,
> Than fly to others that we know not of?

Like all rhetorical questions, Hamlet's queries here are actually statements in disguise. That is, when one asks, with exasperation, 'Well what did you expect to happen when you did X?,' or 'Who walks from here to there in the middle of the night?' one is declaring a position rather than asking for real answers. The force of the questions is to state, respectively, 'You should have known that X would happen (anyone would)!' and 'It is foolish to walk so far at that hour!' Hamlet's rhetorical questions detail **the slings and arrows of outrageous fortune**. He even repeats the form of his earlier metaphor in the phrase **the whips and scorns of time**. His question begins with the word **For**, which, we soon see, introduces a logical explanation for the **must give us pause; there's the respect** line.

We encounter, in the phrase **for who would bear**, an unusually important word: **bear**. Hamlet will use the word twice more in this speech – and perhaps even more than that, when one observes the **bare** of **bare bodkin**, and the buried past tense of **bear** that may appear in **from whose bourn no traveller returns**. Early on in the soliloquy Hamlet has had the opportunity to use this word, but used **suffer** instead. Perhaps he did so because **suffer** best introduces the theme of pain and trouble developed over the first part of the speech. But in the following 13 lines he will speak more specifically of things that we put up with – choose to **suffer** – in life, and so he uses the more general **bear**.

This allows him to extend the walking theme that has come into the speech with **shuffle**. Of course, **bear** can mean merely 'to endure' or 'suffer.' But, as we will see, it can also refer to one carrying a heavy load from one place to another. Hamlet invokes the first meaning – the **suffer** sense – in this section's first seven lines. In them, he writes a morality play of sorts, in which an Everyman figure undergoes the trials of a cruel and unfair life: a morality play without morals. We can read this section as making particular the otherwise generalized metaphors that began the speech: **the slings and arrows of outrageous fortune**, the **sea of troubles**, and **the heart-ache and the thousand natural shocks that flesh is heir to**. Hamlet seems consciously to ease us into the specifics of his list by beginning with **whips and scorns of time**. The echoes here of **slings and arrows of outrageous fortune** link what follows to the earlier section even as they prepare us for another round of restatement or explanation. We can see this shift occurring within the phrase **whips and scorns** itself. That is, where **slings and arrows** offers two parallel weapons (with **sling** standing in for things that a **sling** propels), the phrase **whips and scorns** puts two different kinds of things together. A **whip** is an instrument to cause pain and suffering, just like **slings and arrows** and the **bodkin** that will follow. But **scorns** are something that come from people: mocks, gibes, insults. Joining them with **and**, Hamlet creates a transition between things that hurt the **flesh** and actions (or inactions) that give us **heart-ache**.

The contrast is between things done with physical weapons and things done (sometimes by omission) through human actions, relationships, and institutions. Throughout this section, he ascribes wrongs to persons and personified agents: **time**, **love**, **law**, **office**, **th' unworthy**. In the morality play of life, according to Hamlet, we experience things and individuals acting against us:

time	[wields]	**whips and scorns**
an **oppressor**	[commits]	**wrong**
the proud man	[exhibits]	**contumely**
despis'd love	[brings us]	**pangs**
law	**delay**[s]	[justice or satisfaction]
office	[shows]	**insolence**
th' unworthy	[give]	**spurns** [to] **patient merit**

The schematic morality play represented here features, again, a combination of actions and inactions. Where **time**, an **oppressor**, and **office** *do* things, **love**, **law**, and **th' unworthy** bring suffering by *not* doing things. Although **spurns** seems a potentially active word, the force of **patient** in the phrase **patient merit** connects this idea with the **pangs** and **delay** of **despis'd love** and **law**, respectively. Individually, each of these scenarios describes a wrong that produces **heart-ache** and **suffer**[ing]. Together, they add up to a level of misery that, for Hamlet, has a philosophical force.

We will come to the shape of this philosophical insight shortly, but first let us look at how Hamlet seems to conclude his train of thought: **when he himself might his quietus make with a bare bodkin.** He may add the **himself** here to avoid confusion following the complexity of the previous line: **that patient merit of th' unworthy takes.** Hamlet wants to be clear that the **he** of this next line is the **he** who has experienced the bad things in life that Hamlet has detailed in his catalogue. Hamlet brings this litany to a head, posing a rhetorical question as a forceful appeal: **who** indeed **would bear** all these things – perhaps *any* of these things – if that person could **his quietus make with a bare bodkin**?

The word **quietus** comes from a more formal register than even

question, of which it is certainly a sound-echo and even perhaps a loose anagram. Almost all the letters in **question** reappear in **quietus**, with the leftover letters being 'n' and 'o,' which appropriately spell **no**, the word and theme that preoccupy Hamlet in this soliloquy. The word **quietus** was part of a formal Latin phrase, *quietus est*, used to declare an account 'paid in full,' a debt cleared. Recalling the phrase *consummatum est* noted above in relation to **consummation**, we can sense how Shakespeare and Hamlet are asking us to think about formal conclusions to things. The formal end to a financial relationship — a loan of money or other kind of debt — stands in for the 'debt' we owe to God: our life. (Clearly the kind of debt we are not allowed to clear with money.) The fact that the Elizabethans pronounced 'debt' and 'death' in similar ways allowed Shakespeare to pun on the words' relationship in many of his works.

His logic in this section of the soliloquy follows the kind of reasoning one encounters in the 'syllogisms' popular in Elizabethan schoolbooks. A familiar form goes as follows: All men are mortal; Socrates is a man; therefore Socrates is mortal. Hamlet's reasoning is never tidy, but we can see that it follows an initial chain here:

We seek the good.

To have an end of troubles is good.

Therefore we should seek an end of troubles.

We have already considered Hamlet's catalogue of the **sea of troubles** that life brings us. To be in society is to **suffer** from its institutions, including the **law**, high **office**, and any powerful **oppressor**. To be human is to **suffer** unrequited **love**, the **whips and scorns of time**, the **contumely** of the **proud man** and the **spurns** of **th' unworthy**. **Contumely** means contempt or scorn, and the kind of treatment that accompanies such contempt. Hamlet knows as well as anyone that these rise to the level of profound **troubles** and together can make life miserable. Yet he has, as early as the phrase **perchance to**

dream, recognized that the ultimate problem is not with the **sea of troubles**. The ultimate problem lies with the idea of the **end**, a word and concept that, as we have seen, have appeared throughout the soliloquy not only in the word **end** but in **die, sleep** (provisionally), **consummation, shuffled off**, and **quietus**.

The **rub**, or blocking point, to Hamlet lies in the possibility that death will not **end** our troubles. We could phrase his doubt as follows:

To have an end of troubles is good.

But it is not certain that the end of life brings an end of troubles.

Therefore we should not end our life.

As we have seen, every rhetorical question disguises (however thinly) a statement (in *Hamlet*, the reverse may be true as well). The statement Hamlet makes here is that 'Life is indeed miserable.' This statement comes in support of Hamlet's thinking about life, death, and misery. But we should be careful to observe his conclusion: while to be done with troubles is **devoutly to be wish'd**, the nature of the **dreams** that **may come** after death gives us **pause** in hoping for a quicker end to our **heart-ache**.

The next part of his extended rhetorical question restates this beginning even as it adds to it. When Hamlet asks **who would fardels bear** he makes more concrete the **bear** with which he began (**for who would bear the whips and scorns of time**). A **fardel** is a burden. Where **bear** had meant merely **suffer**, Hamlet now invites us to imagine ourselves loaded down with a heavy pack or burden. Burdened, we **grunt and sweat under a weary life**. The word **under** here means, first, 'in the context of,' 'while experiencing or conducting.' Like a person struggling under a heavy load, we live a **weary life** while shouldering the **fardels** of our **troubles**. But just as **so long life** hinted that **life** itself was *too* **long**, the word **under** smuggles in an image of an **oppressor** (perhaps a personified **life**) adding to our burden by weighing things down. It is almost as though **life** were perching atop the pack that we **bear**, or were the baggage that we carry. We might think here of Atlas struggling under the weight of the Earth – an image traditionally believed to have been painted over the entrance to the Globe Playhouse. The first part of this section looked back to **the respect** for its conclusion; the question becomes rhetorical because this answer is known in advance. The next section of the soliloquy, in contrast, depends on what comes later in the question.

In its most compact form, what follows supplies a rationale: **but that the dread of something after death ... puzzles the will.** Hamlet has earlier spoken of the **sleep of death**, raising the possibility that if we **dream**, those **dreams** may be horrifying, more troubling than the **sea of troubles** we experience in life. His return to the subject of the afterlife is less explicit here – **something after death** – even as he grows clearer about the feeling one experiences: **dread**. This sensation delivers a stronger way of putting things than **must give us pause**, of course. Hamlet's more specific language may come from his pondering the middle section of this passage: **the undiscover'd country, from whose bourn no traveller returns.** Earlier, again, he has imagined **death** as **sleep**. With the metaphors of movement and walking that have crept into his speech – we could consider **shuffled off** and the picture of someone **grunt**ing and **sweat**ing while **bear**ing a heavy load – Hamlet now imagines **death** as a kind of journey. Taken by all mortal things, this journey is to a destination we know nothing about. The afterlife is thus an **undiscover'd country** the same way a country or continent is not **discover'd** until a **traveller** brings back news of its existence and details about its landscape or residents. The word **bourn** means 'boundary' or 'frontier,' and may signify here the general region of death – whether we imagine it to be Heaven, the Elysian Fields, or something else. We have already seen that this word echoes the **bear/bare** pairing (he will use the former word again presently) and ironically gestures toward the land of **death** with a word commonly connected with birth.

The phrase **puzzles the will** perfectly describes one understanding of Hamlet's situation in the play as well as one of the effects his speech has on its readers and listeners. The strong verb **puzzles** suggests bewilderment, being so baffled that one's **will** — the place or faculty of self-determination — cannot function. This state of inaction means we accept things as they are, however unbearable they may seem. The **dread** of an unknown **something after death** not only **puzzles the will**, but in so doing **makes us rather bear those ills we have than fly to others that we know not of.** That is, we endure the evils that we have as preferable to **ills** we can only imagine. We could note that Hamlet's metaphors of movement have so increased their energy that now he imagines that we do not **shuffle** or trudge while **bear**ing a burden, but **fly** (that is, rush or hasten) toward a destination. It is as though he pictures us throwing off our heavy load of **fardels** and, newly lightened, hurrying toward loads that may be even heavier.

Hamlet's tendency to restate, characterize, and sum up continues in the speech's next sentence, which begins with the connective word **Thus**. The fact that we do not — cannot — know what comes after death both **give**s **us pause** and, more strongly, **puzzles the will.** We accept the status quo for fear that the irreversible change of our death may be a change for the worse. No one knows, for no one has returned — can return — from **the undiscover'd country.** As Hamlet continues, he attributes this fear to **conscience: Thus conscience does make cowards of us all.** With **conscience**, Hamlet doubtless refers to our innermost thoughts, the voice inside us that speaks to us as though in conversation. It can also refer to the very capacity to know, and to know oneself. Perhaps the internalized voice of **conscience** comes with some irony, counterpoising the theme of heroically taking **arms against a sea of troubles.** Certainly from a heroic point of view any **dread** would indeed **make cowards** of those who acted out of fear rather than bravery. Only one who believes in heroism has the confidence to label another person a **coward**, and Hamlet may use a hero's voice to disparage our fear to act.

We may well hear this heroic strain in the longer, repeated version of this line when Hamlet continues **and thus the native hue of resolution is sicklied o'er with the pale cast of thought ...** By **native**, Hamlet refers to that which is innate or instinctive: we are *naturally* disposed to act, he implies. A **hue of resolution** is a metaphor that combines our innate appearance or complexion (**hue**) with another attribute, that of **resolution** – the resolve to do things, which the **puzzled will** does not do out of **dread** and a **coward**ly **conscience**. Shakespeare combines **hue** and **resolution** so Hamlet can set up a double contrast:

pale	is to	**native hue**
	as	
cast of thought	is to	**resolution**

With its unusual verb, the phrase **sicklied o'er** presents an image of an otherwise healthy-looking **resolution** – naturally healthy, the word **native** suggests – made sick-looking by the **pale cast of thought**. We may hear, too, in the close conjunction of **o'er** and **cast** a buried metaphor (that of an 'overcast' or cloudy day) that adds to the effectiveness of the larger image. Taken as a whole, Hamlet's sentence suggests the sickly eclipse of health by doubt.

Hamlet has begun to criticize himself – and **us all** as well – in this **Thus** section. But the heroic strain becomes most alive in the concluding lines of the speech: **And enterprises of great pitch and moment with this regard their currents turn awry, and lose the name of action.** We can hear an echo of **slings and arrows of outrageous fortune** in the phrase **enterprises of great pitch and moment**, which reverses the order of the earlier phrasing. This resemblance seems more than accidental, for **enterprises** are things to be done, just as the first section of the soliloquy saw the counterpoint of **suffer**ing the **slings and arrows of outrageous fortune** as being the taking up of **arms against a sea of troubles**. In the next chapter, we will look more closely at the heroic register of these words. But for now, it is enough to say that the **enterprises** Hamlet describes are no ordinary ones. He uses the doubled phrase **of great pitch and moment** to magnify the importance of his subject. The word **pitch** can mean 'height,' and had a special application in the sport of falconry, where it described the highest part of a hawk or falcon's flight just before swooping down on its prey. The word **moment**, for its part, signifies 'importance' or 'consequence' and has within it earlier senses (from Latin and Romance languages) of both weight and movement – even weight that implies or entails movement.

The phrase **with this regard** recalls for us **there's the respect**, and means 'in the face of this fact' or 'in consideration thereof.' It will be important to notice that, so thoroughly has the heroic register of speech taken over Hamlet's diction, the **enterprises of great pitch and moment** cannot be described as overcome by things external to them. Instead, they are like rushing rivers that decide *on their own* to seek another channel: **with this regard their currents turn awry**. Hamlet has earlier asked us to imagine the fanciful (if heroic) scene of someone taking **arms against a sea of troubles**. Here his water metaphor finds expression so strongly that we may not notice who or what is doing the acting. The **enterprise**-rivers **turn ... their currents ... awry**, that is, aside, with the suggestion of error or mistake. By doing so, they **lose the name of action**. Here **name** most likely means 'credit' or 'honor,' suggesting that in **turn**ing **awry** from their original goals, the **moment**ous **enterprises** have lost any capital (including honor, reputation, fame, and renown) that they could have gained by staying the course. The word **name** may also convey the simpler sense of what something is called, and we will remember how important **name**s are to all Shakespeare's characters.

We could take the concluding words of Hamlet's soliloquy as **Soft you now, the fair Ophelia**. Although technically they mark a departure from his main topic, they seem, like his other words and unlike the lines that immediately follow them, to be addressed to himself. In particular, they may recall that part of Hamlet who stands outside himself (or inside himself, like **conscience**) and says such things as **no more** and **ay, there's the rub**. As we will see at more length in the next chapter of this book, though, he introduces the word **you** for the first time in these lines, perhaps because someone very important to him on a personal level has drawn his attention. It is easy to speak of **we** and **us** when philosophizing; it is difficult not to speak personally when speaking of love. The word **Soft** here works primarily as a command. With it, Hamlet tells himself (**you**) to 'hold on,' or 'wait a moment.' But it also combines with the word **fair** and the name **Ophelia** to make his speech end with a suggestion of the pleasant, tender, and personal. The introduction of self-reference here (**you**) as well as the invocation of another (**Ophelia**) effectively marks the end of the soliloquy by changing its language.

Throughout this soliloquy we have heard Hamlet restating what he has said. These restatements often make things less – rather than more – clear. Paraphrase, saying things again in a different way, always runs this risk, for different words take us to different places. Good readers have long resisted paraphrases of poetry, for poetry often succeeds precisely by being less than clear to begin with. That is, it can strive to say not one thing only, but many. Changing a poet's words can shut down meaning even as we seek to clarify it.

Hamlet's 'To be or not to be' soliloquy is a prime instance of a poem that says many things at the same time. So paraphrasing it means reducing that complexity. But in the interest of making concrete at least one possible reading among the many we have explored here, it may be helpful to repeat it, in modern language, from start to finish:

> To be, or not to be, that is the question:
> Whether it's better to suffer in one's head
> The outrageous wrongs that life brings us,
> Or to take matters in our own hands and oppose

These troubles, thus ending them. To die may be
Like sleeping; and perhaps this sleep would end
The heart-ache and thousand pains that come
With being alive; if that were true, it would be something
To wish for indeed. But if we say dying is like sleeping,
That sleep may bring dreams. Yes, that's the problem,
For in that sleep of death the kind of dreams that may come,
When we have shuffled our way off this troubling planet,
Must make us stop and think. There's the painful fact
That makes our long lives so troubling:
For who would bear the torments that come over time –
Being wronged by those in power, looked down on by the
        proud,
The broken hearts of unrequited love, injustice,
The arrogance of bureaucrats, and the stuff we put up with
Patiently from those who aren't worthy in any way –
When we could put an end to all this by killing ourselves
With a nice knife? Who would carry this load,
Grunting and sweating through this weary life,
If it weren't the case that the fear of something after death
(That place we know nothing about, for no one has
Ever returned from the grave) freezes us into inaction,
Making us accept the ills that we have rather
Than to rush toward those we know nothing about?
Conscience makes cowards of all of us this way,
And the innate capacity we have to do things
Is made ineffective by our thinking too much;
The great things we could do
Are also diverted by this,
And lose the chance for acting. – But hold on,
Here's the fair Ophelia.

An immediate and sincere apology is called for. This paraphrase attempts to preserve the visual aspects of the soliloquy in a line-for-line restatement, but obviously loses Shakespeare's poetry when it discards Hamlet's metaphors, imagery, and word-music. When compared with the plodding language above, the original speech's quality becomes even more apparent. For instance, trading a phrase like **native hue of resolution** for 'innate capacity we have to do things' means sacrificing creative brilliance for plain, even ugly restatement.

Paraphrasing this speech asks us to make choices among the many possibilities we saw for most of its lines, phrases, and even words. Truth be told, the speech could have been paraphrased in hundreds of different ways, each of which would offer a different interpretation through its choice of words, images, and emphasis. One thing not fully addressed by keeping the speech's initial words is the long-standing belief that this is a suicide speech. It is important to recognize that Hamlet proposes suicide clearly only one time in his soliloquy: in lines 74–5, when he says **when he himself might his quietus make with a bare bodkin.** Many readers shift this instance to account for more generalized passages earlier and later in the speech. Perhaps this is unavoidable, and even a part of the speech's mystery. That is, because the soliloquy is so puzzling, it tempts us to find a word, experience, thought, or action that will explain things, once for all – and in a conclusive way. Thus saying 'it is a speech about suicide' seems to put a **quietus** of our own on the soliloquy's difficulties.

Attending to the contours of the speech as written and delivered shows us that if this is a speech 'about' suicide, it is also about other things – things even more terrifying than that subject (and which in fact scare us out of thoughts of ending our lives). In fact, we could draw a useful analogy between this soliloquy and the frightful head of Medusa that populates so many Renaissance books and paintings. Like the horrifying visage of this monstrous, snake-haired Gorgon, the 'To be or not to be' soliloquy has the power to 'freeze' those who encounter it. As Macduff puts it after coming across the corpse of Duncan, 'Approach the chamber, and destroy your sight / With a new Gorgon' (*Macbeth* 2.3.71–2). As the following pages mean to show, Hamlet's soliloquy stuns us in a similar way, chilling us with its cold images and rhythms. Yet it does so less suddenly than what Macduff sees, working its fearful magic through the ebbs and flows of intellectual activity.

If there is one thing this formidable speech does well – and it does many things well – it is to introduce us to the *process* of its speaker's thoughts, thoughts that admittedly take many forms in this play. As we will see, the 'To be or not to be' soliloquy asks us to participate in Hamlet's logic, his way of seeing the world. It also leads us to feel what he and other characters in the play experience. To get to the sometimes terrifying logic and experience represented by the speech, the next chapter of this book takes up not the speech's *what* but its *how*, examining the soliloquy as a kind of poem.

To be or not to be

To be, or not to be, that is the question: 55
Whether 'tis nobler in the mind to suffer
The slings and arrows of outrageous fortune,
Or to take arms against a sea of troubles,
And by opposing, end them. To die, to sleep –
No more, and by a sleep to say we end 60
The heart-ache and the thousand natural shocks
That flesh is heir to; 'tis a consummation
Devoutly to be wish'd. To die, to sleep –
To sleep, perchance to dream – ay, there's the rub,
For in that sleep of death what dreams may come, 65
When we have shuffled off this mortal coil,
Must give us pause; there's the respect
That makes calamity of so long life:
For who would bear the whips and scorns of time,
Th' oppressor's wrong, the proud man's contumely, 70
The pangs of despis'd love, the law's delay,
The insolence of office, and the spurns
That patient merit of th' unworthy takes,
When he himself might his quietus make
With a bare bodkin; who would fardels bear, 75
To grunt and sweat under a weary life,
But that the dread of something after death,
The undiscover'd country, from whose bourn
No traveller returns, puzzles the will,
And makes us rather bear those ills we have, 80
Than fly to others that we know not of?
Thus conscience does make cowards of us all,
And thus the native hue of resolution
Is sicklied o'er with the pale cast of thought,
And enterprises of great pitch and moment 85
With this regard their currents turn awry,
And lose the name of action. – Soft you now,
The fair Ophelia.

4 How Does it Mean? (The Speech as Poem)

Looking at *what* Hamlet's speech means, we were forced to confront *how* it means. We observed, for instance, its continual restatements and its clarifications that only made things more complex. We saw that its famous first line has a cleverly balanced architecture, dividing in half with each of its halves dividing that way again. We saw the soliloquy mixing homely words like **rub** and **fardels** with academic terms, such as **question** and **respect**, with religious words, such as **consummation** and **devoutly**, and even the commercial-legalistic **quietus**. Along the way, we saw that these and other elements could not be separated from the meaning of the speech. If our awkward paraphrase of the speech showed anything, it is that what Hamlet says cannot be distinguished from the manner in which he says it. The words, phrases, lines, images, sounds, and structures are not only the means through which his speech works; they are the speech itself. Outside them, it does not exist.

If the *how* of Hamlet's speech continually crept into our attempt to understand its meaning, we will also find out that the reverse is true. The *what* of 'To be or not to be' invariably comes into play when we turn to questions of form and structure, as will issues of performance and story. Where we began our quest for meaning by reading the speech in slow motion, as it were, an analysis of how it works will need to cut back and forth between 'close ups' and 'framing shots.' We will alternate focusing on such things as specific words and sounds with consideration of larger elements like form and genre.

We could begin by pointing out the obvious: the 'To be or not to be' speech is a *soliloquy*. Like almost everything connected with what Hamlet says and does, however, even this observation has been challenged. As we will see in the next chapter of this book, some believe that other characters overhear Hamlet as he speaks, and others believe that he is both overheard and aware of this. Still others feel that he speaks his speech *intending* to be overheard. Whatever the case may be, it can help to start with a definition. The term 'soliloquy' comes from Latin *solus* (alone) + *loqui* (to speak), and commonly refers to dramatic speeches delivered by a character in solitude. To those who talk to themselves on a daily basis, the convention of dramatic characters speaking alone may not in itself seem unusual. What is different, of course, is that those of us who speak to ourselves rarely rise above muttering, while the characters of Shakespeare and his contemporary playwrights are typically quite eloquent in their soliloquies. Seemingly trained (as were most of the playwrights) in the arts of rhetoric, they commonly announce a problem or topic and work through it thoughtfully in a kind of dialogue with themselves. Often they conclude a formal speech – however productively – with a 'capping couplet' (that is, two lines of rhyming verse) that seems to signal a recognized end to their train of thought and speech. The capping couplet may also have had a theatrical purpose, announcing to the next actor who speaks that it is time for him to enter and/or begin delivering his lines.

Hamlet delivers a number of soliloquies: six or seven, depending on how one counts them. Four of these finish with capping couplets, such as 'O, what a rogue and peasant slave am I!', which ends with the well-known lines 'the play's the thing / Wherein I'll catch the conscience of the King' (2.2.604–5). For various reasons, the 'To be or not to be' soliloquy does not end so tidily. For one thing, Hamlet is interrupted by (or interrupts himself to notice) Ophelia, who occupies a position on stage as well as in the final lines of his speech. Perhaps the speech could not end neatly for thematic reasons as well. Settling upon the reality of our all too human fears, Hamlet cannot wrap them up with a bow the way he is able to with some of his other speeches. In addition to the 'conscience of the King'ending, he gives us:

How in my words somever she be shent,
To give them seals never my soul consent!

(3.2.398–9)

My mother stays,
This physic but prolongs thy sickly days.

(3.3.95–6)

O, from this time forth,
My thoughts be bloody, or be nothing worth!

(4.4.65–6)

Unlike these soliloquies, Hamlet's 'To be or not to be' speech is interrupted, and concludes not by gaining a rhyme but with an acknowledgement of *loss*: **and lose the name of action**.

These couplets show us something important about soliloquies: they are typically quite personal. One could notice the personal references in the lines quoted above: '*I'll* catch the conscience;' '*my* words' and '*my* soul;' '*My* mother;' '*My* thoughts.' Turning to 'To be or not to be,' we notice a surprising fact. Unlike every one of his other soliloquies, Hamlet's 'To be or not to be' speech uses no first person pronouns: no *I*, no *me*, no *my* or *mine*. When he speaks directly to Ophelia to end the soliloquy, he says, of course, 'Nymph, in thy orisons be all my sins remembered' (this line follows the materials we ended with in the previous chapter). But in the heart of the speech recognized as his most famous soliloquy, a literary form that all but defines the personal, we encounter a strangely *im*personal choice of words. Hamlet says, for instance, **when we have shuffled off this**

mortal coil, that this gives **us pause**, that a hypothetical *he* would be likely to commit suicide, that this **make *us* rather bear the ills *we* have than fly to others that *we* know not of**, that **conscience does make cowards of *us* all**. In each of his sentences, Hamlet has the opportunity to personalize his remarks. He declines to do so, instead generalizing what he says so that it applies to **us all**.

This strangely impersonal cast to his soliloquy is one of the things that make it float above the rest of the play. He speaks in the general language of philosophy about deeply human matters. It is possible, of course, to apply various subjects in his soliloquy to specific parts of his dramatic 'life.' Thus **the insolence of office**, for example, could be taken to refer to Claudius's arrogant assumption of and behavior in the 'office' of King. But to search for such individualized applications in Hamlet's speech seems to go against its grain. Throughout, he strenuously avoids referring to himself. This, again, contrasts with what he does in every other soliloquy he utters. We could consider such lines as (to give only these): 'no more like my father / Than I to Hercules' (1.2.152–3); 'And shall I couple hell?' (1.4.93); 'Why, what an ass am I!' (2.2.582); 'Now could I drink hot blood' (3.2.390); 'How all occasions do inform against me, / And spur my dull revenge!' (4.4.32–3). These examples confirm our sense that Hamlet's soliloquies tend to be intensely personal. And while we have seen Hamlet appearing to step outside himself to say **no more** and **there's the rub**, this uttering of asides does not translate into declaring himself the subject of his speech.

The 'To be or not to be' soliloquy – perhaps the most resonant presentation of the personal in all of literature – achieves this resonance in part by avoiding reference to Hamlet's own person. Shakespeare makes Hamlet's concerns available to readers and audience members by strategically using pronouns (**we**, **us**, and **he**) that allow Hamlet to speak for us. Calling the soliloquy a 'secular prayer' may not do justice to its philosophical and dramatic textures, but this label does succeed in capturing its resemblance to a prayer's script-like openness. The speech itself is followed closely by references to Ophelia's own prayers: her 'orisons.' Save for actors portraying these characters, no one repeats the lines of Horatio, Malvolio, or Pistol on a regular basis. Yet, like the Lord's Prayer ('*Our* Father . . . *our* daily bread'), Hamlet's soliloquy is repeated somewhere on earth daily. Unlike his more personal soliloquies, which have his character and the play's plot inscribed on their surfaces, the 'To be or not to be' soliloquy shares with most prayers a general applicability. Anyone can insert him/herself into the speech because Hamlet avoids talking only about himself.

Six working parts define the soliloquy. As we will see, each of these parts contributes something different and significant to the speech:

1. **To be, or not to be** *through* **opposing, end them.** (4.8 lines; 39 words)
2. **To die, to sleep** *through* **devoutly to be wish'd.** (4 lines; 33 words)
3. **To die, to sleep** *through* **so long life:** (5.4 lines; 45 words)

---

4. **For who would bear** *through* **bare bodkin**; (6.5 lines; 50 words)
5. **who would fardels** *through* **we know not of?** (6.5 lines; 51 words)
6. **Thus conscience** *through* **The fair Ophelia.** (6.5 lines; 50 words)

There are of course several other ways to divide the soliloquy, but this division captures its primary units of thought and expression. It especially indicates the even balance of what we could call Hamlet's 'thought paragraphs,' the building blocks of his soliloquy. We could note that each of his soliloquy's parts falls between four lines and six-and-a-half lines, and uses between 33 and 51 words. Even though they mirror each other in structure and theme, it is surely an accident that sections 4 and 5 of the soliloquy as divided above occupy exactly the same number of lines and use almost the same number of words. But that accident reinforces our sense of the symmetry we have seen at work as early as the first line, with its compellingly balanced architecture.

Glancing at this division, we can see that repetition is key to the speech. We have already noted the deep symmetry of the soliloquy's opening lines, and it seems clear that this symmetry continues throughout the speech in the form of repeated words, ideas, and structures. To begin with the most apparent structural repetition, we could note that in the division above the three parts are balanced in each of the speech's halves. Several of the sections repeat (both internally and externally) various words, phrases, and ideas. We have the repetition of **To be ... to be** with **To die, to sleep ... to be wish'd** and **To die, to sleep**; the second half witnesses the repetition of **For who would bear** in the punning **bare** of **bare bodkin**, as well as the doubling of this opening question in the second query, **who would fardels**.

Within such instances of balance as well as between the speech's sections, we encounter a peculiar, almost hypnotic rhythm. This rhythm will be one of the keys to the speech's 'mystery,' as it were. Anyone who has ever spoken the soliloquy's initial line senses that it begins with a back-and-forth movement: **To be, or not to be**. It is easy to feel the swing from **To be**, to its opposite, **not to be**. The speech begins, then, almost like an antique clock, with its pendulum-like movement marking the dwindling minutes of our existence with its balanced alternatives. This ebb-and-flow feeling will characterize many moments in the speech, with a movement out balanced by an equal pulling back. We sense this, for instance, in the balance of the **whether** clause, and in the rhetorical questions that answer themselves: **For who ... when** and **who would ... but**.

We could also see the famous first line as taking its balanced structure from the morality play, a form we noticed in the last chapter when we examined the afflicted journey that Hamlet's imagined human takes through life. One of the common features of the English morality play was a debate-like confrontation between two entities – *Doctor Faustus* represents them as a 'Good Angel' and an 'Evil Angel' – who actively struggle for the protagonist's soul. The technical name for this struggle is *psychomachia*, literally a war for the psyche or soul. Where Faustus's angels stand on either side of him to make their cases (he is wooed one way and then the other), Hamlet's **To be / not to be** division internalizes this debate structure: the twin angels are no longer outside our protagonist; they are between his ears and in his soul.

But these images – the pendulum and psychomachia – can only take us so far. For one of the things that makes this soliloquy so peculiar is that it introduces us to a series of pairs, only to ask us to imagine a third item. Instead of 'item,' here, we should say 'place,' for the experience of reading, listening to, and even speaking the 'To be or not to be' soliloquy is like moving quickly and even uncertainly from one place to another. Hamlet has himself given us a version of this rapid movement in Act 1, Scene 5, when he moves Horatio and the soldiers around on stage in response to the voice of his father's Ghost booming from below: *'Hic et ubique?* Then we'll shift our ground' (156). Like the Latin question here, 'To be or not to be' takes us 'Here and everywhere.' We could compare it to leaping among the mossy stones of a fast-moving stream at dusk. Standing on the phrase **To be**, we jump fairly confidently to another spot, **not to be**. Rather than returning safely to the comfort of the original spot, or (even better) landing with both feet squarely on each stone, we find that the line's end, **that is the question**, makes us leap to yet another rock. When we encounter the **whether** clause, we repeat this motion, all the time moving forward, and are forced to land on yet another third space with **end them**. We follow out the steps of this risky game all over again with **To die** and **to sleep**, this time stepping twice on **to sleep**, before hopping to another rock with **perchance to dream**. So we continue, moving downstream uneasily. At the speech's midpoint we begin to take comfort in the resumed, easy, back-and-forth of the catalogue: **oppressor's wrong** is one stone, **proud man's contumely** another, and so on through **bare bodkin**.

We start to repeat these motions when Hamlet begins this question all over again, but then he changes the rules of the game. The phrase

weary life leads us to think that a new catalogue is starting, but this is not the case. We are relieved to sense that **life** and **death** are an easy pair – a step here, a step there – but **country** abandons the pair pattern and gives us four verbs in a row, with each new step harder to make: **returns … puzzles … makes … fly**. The easy pair of **conscience does make** and **resolution is sicklied** lulls us into false confidence once again, but this gives way to an **and** pattern: **and thus … and enterprises … turn … and lose …** Just as we have mastered this, the speech suddenly asks us to leap in an entirely new direction: **Soft you now, the fair Ophelia**. And a new game begins.

Before we proceed, we could return to something we have only touched upon in the breakdown above. That is, the abundance of the word **to** in the first three sections. Like the intensive pairing and repetition in the soliloquy generally, **to** is partnered with many other words. The soliloquy features 13 instances of the word **to** prior to **there's the rub**, and only two after that (in one case, in the phrase **than fly to others**). Only one of these initial uses is not the infinitive or verbal **to** (the phrase **That flesh is heir to**). We could illustrate this feature as follows:

	be
	not be
	suffer
	take arms
	die
	sleep
TO	say
	be wish'd
	die
	sleep
	sleep
	dream

Why this preference for **to** forms in the first third of the soliloquy, and why does it fall off after this point? Perhaps Hamlet uses the **to** form not only because this word helps describe action, but because **to** renders that action strikingly impersonal. Such impersonality characterizes a later use of this form in his speech, when he asks, for example, who would choose **to grunt and sweat under a weary life**. We could notice that he is doubly impersonal: *a* **weary life**. It is the life of not only the unidentified **who**, but anyone. Hamlet's use of the **to** form allows him to capture the very kind of impersonality we employ, for instance, in such proverbial sayings as 'To err is human; to forgive, divine,' and in giving directions: 'To get to The Fishes pub, take the Willow Walk just south of Botley Road Park.' Each of these sentences remains open for anyone to step in and perform its action (erring, forgiving, walking). In the same way, the first third of Hamlet's soliloquy offers a menu of actions. As we have seen, the speech slowly closes this menu, ultimately withdrawing it at **and lose the name of action**.

We will take up the role of repetition in these sections, and in the speech as a whole, in a moment. First, though, we should ask what Hamlet seeks to accomplish with each part of his speech. The first section clearly introduces alternatives, and goes on, with its **whether** clause, to define those alternatives (however mysterious the definitions are). The **end** of the first section's final line seems to prompt the **sleep of death** analogy taken up in the second, a section that concludes by stating the desirability of ending things without further trouble. As though nagged by doubt that such an easy conclusion could be possible, Hamlet returns to the **sleep of death** analogy with the exact same words of the previous section: **To die, to sleep**. In this third section, though, he concludes that his first answer was too easy, for our **dreams** may be even more troubling than our **long life**. The next two sections ask rhetorical questions – **For who would ... ?** – that work to intensify his earlier indictment of life's **sea of troubles** even as they lead to a larger, more formal conclusion about our human fears. With its two uses of **thus**, the sixth section of his speech summarizes why we **lose the name of action**, allowing **enterprises of great pitch and moment** to **turn awry**. Noticing Ophelia's presence, Hamlet closes his train of thought with self-address: **Soft you now, the fair Ophelia**.

One of the key things we have begun to notice about the structure of Hamlet's soliloquy is how much it employs repetition. Clearly we remember the speech by its famous first words, which give us the repetition with a difference of **To be, or not to be**. A version of this kind of repetition appears in the speech's many **and** phrases, such as **slings and arrows**, **whips and scorns**, **grunt and sweat**, and **pitch and moment**. At first we may see these pairings as very different from **To be, or not to be**. Using **and** rather than **or**, for instance, they avoid the negation of the first line to offer us similar things. Although logically each member of the pairings can be distinguished from one another − a **sling** differs from an **arrow**, **whips** from **scorns**, and so forth − they fall so closely in Hamlet's vision and so quickly in his speech that they come close to redundancy. These phrases are almost unnecessarily repetitious, as though a kind of rhetorical overkill.

In this repetition, they perhaps ask us to see the phrase **To be, or not to be** differently. Rather than *only* a balanced alternative, this famous phrase could be read as combining as well as separating its items. Such, at least, is one implication of the line's end: **that is the question**. Seeing this introductory phrase as joining in addition to distinguishing its possibilities allows us to hold it as a part of Hamlet's habit, in this speech, of thinking in pairs that are neither the same nor absolutely different. Is being all that different from not being? Can we be more certain about one than the other? This was, in fact, the burden of our diagram in the book's last chapter, where we saw that the stoic and heroic interpretations of the **whether** clause criss-crossed, not only logically but also verbally, with the soliloquy's famous opening line.

Other kinds of repetition lend the soliloquy an intricate patterning as well. Hamlet repeats the phrase **To die, to sleep** verbatim, for instance, and then repeats **to sleep** a third time, only to qualify it with a further option: **to dream.** He repeats the word **for** in the lines **for in that sleep of death** and **for who would bear,** and continues to chain his lines by repeating the latter's **who** and **bear** in the phrase **who would fardels bear.** We have already noticed the uncanny repetition of **bear,** in various forms, in the speech. Earlier, we noticed as well the repetition of the *m* . . . *k* beginning in *m*a**ke cowards** and *m*a**kes calamity.** To these, we could add **dreams may come,** *m*o**rtal coil,** and *m*a**n's contumely.** We could also observe lingering if inexact echoes of this cluster in such phrases as *m*o**ment** . . . **currents,** *q*u**ie-tus** *m*a**ke,** and **na***m*e . . . **action,** and note its exact inversion in such words and phrases as **consu***m*m**ation, contu***m*e**ly,** and **conscience** . . . **make,** as well as within the very word *m*a**ke** itself. The repetition of soft 'm' and hard 'c'/'k' sounds here could be seen as the sonic equivalent of the opposites we get in **be** and **not . . . be.**

These dozen or so instances of *m* . . . *k* and its inversion could lead us to declare this arrangement of consonants as something like the 'secret sound' of 'To be or not to be.' It may be an accident that so many words and phrases in this short speech deploy this sound cluster, backwards and forwards. But it could have been more than that. The author of *Hamlet* – a writer who sometimes puckishly played with the names of not only family and friends in his works but his own – would have been used to joining these very sounds every time he said his name: 'willia**M** sha**K**espeare.' So when we hear *m*o**rtal coil** and other such pairings of these consonants, we may be hearing an echo (however deliberate) of the playwright's name: a kind of sonic signature at the heart of his signature soliloquy.

We noted that this speech does not conclude, as several of Hamlet's soliloquies do, with rhyming lines. But rhymes of a different sort add a poetic dimension to his speech, including repeated sounds within lines, such as **sl***ee***p** and **dr***ea***m,** **h***ue* **of resol***u***tion,** and *of of***ice**; sounds repeated at the ends of lines, such as **takes** and **make**; and those more loosely related, such as **the will** and **those ills**, which resonate both in their 'th' and 'ill' sounds. Early on in the speech, we get a version of *n*ot to *b*e in the next line's **no*b*ler**, and the repetition of sounds such as what we have in **s*l*eep** and **s*ay*** is not uncommon in the speech, as one can see from such phrases as **shuff*l*ed off**, **opp*r*essor's ... *pr*oud**, *l*ove and *l*aw, and **c*o*nscience** and **c*o*wards**, to cite only these.

In addition to these sounds, the speech's words affect us in other ways as well. Counting the compound heart-ache as a single word, we could say that the speech has 267 words, many of them used more than one time. As could be expected, such words as **the** (22), **of** (15), **to** (15), **and** (12), **that** (7), and **a** (5) appear most frequently. But after that, the frequency of some words may surprise us. For instance, Hamlet uses **sleep** five times, and **we** four times; **death** and **life** each appear twice, as do (among others) **die** and **died**, **end**, **makes** and **make, who, would, thus**, and both **no** and **not**.

We will return to these last two words, but for now we should notice that the speech mixes shorter and longer words to great effect. The initial nine words of its famous first line, for instance, have a single syllable each: **To be, or not to be that is the** ... Then we get **question**, which was probably pronounced with two syllables – **QUEST-ion** – rather than with three as in **qui-E-tus** (that is, 'qui-*A Y*-tus') or **QUI-e-tus**. Throughout, the 'To be or not to be' soliloquy alternates the simple diction of ordinary life with the more complex Latinate vocabulary of the learned orders. We can see this in Hamlet's use of both **there's the rub** and the terms **respect, regard, consummation**, and **resolution** to discuss the business of deciding upon action and the ins and outs of action itself. Examining these shorter, simpler words over and against their more elaborate cousins helps reveal one source of the speech's strength. Here are a few of the soliloquy's shorter words, followed in parentheses by the number of times they appear in the soliloquy:

Short Words

> **a** (5); **and** (12); **ay** (1); **be** (3); **but** (1); **by** (2); **die** (2); **for** (2); **have** (2); **he** (1); **his** (1); **in** (2); **is** (3); **may** (1); **of** (15); **or** (2); **say (1); so** (1); **that** (7); **the** (22); **this** (2); **those** (1); **thus** (2); **'tis** (2); **to** (15); **us** (3); **we** (4); **who** (2); **with** (3); **would** (2); **you** (1)

We could contrast the above with some of the words of two or more syllables in the soliloquy, each of which is used only once:

Longer Words

> **calamity; conscience; consummation; contumely; devoutly; enterprises; insolence; natural; Ophelia; opposing; oppressor; outrageous; question; quietus; resolution; traveller; undiscover'd; unworthy**

Hamlet often sets these long and short words in opposition. Just as we have seen **question** stand out at the end of its line (in fact, it makes the line 'irregular' by exceeding ten syllables), he will begin a line **That flesh is heir to; 'tis a** only to end it with **consummation**. In the same way **the proud man's** balances **contumely**, the phrase **native hue of** precedes **resolution**, and **enterprises** is followed by **of great pitch and moment**. We could take this as the verbal side of the speech's pendulum-like movement. Just as the $m \ldots k$ pairing balances through consonants what the first line does with logic, so do these shorter and longer words offer a patterned contrast that works upon the listener in a fairly unconscious way.

The words of the soliloquy fall into a number of overlapping thematic categories. There are many ways to define these themes, of course, and most of the speech's words involve more than one grouping. For instance, we have seen that **rub** comes from the realm of pastimes and

games. Hamlet uses this bowling ball or other object that blocks the
way as a metaphor for a logical impediment. But as a projectile
(something to be thrown by hand) we could also see it as analogous to
arms, slings and arrows, whips and scorns, and **bodkin** – a kind
of hand property, that is, in Hamlet's imaginary theater. Or we could
choose to see **rub** in terms of the debate words (**question, respect,
regard, thus**) that come up time and again in the speech. Thus each
word may fall into several of many dozens of thematic categories that
organize the speech. The following seem primary among these categories: TROUBLE; HESITATION, ERROR, and UNCERTAINTY;
THE BODY; DEATH and ENDINGS; THOUGHT; THE LAW,
DEBATE, and OFFICE; and WEAPONS. Below are the categories
represented in columns, with their various terms:

Trouble

ache (from **heart-
ache**)
against
calamity
coil
contumely
despis'd
die
dread
fortune
grunt
ills
insolence
lose
mortal
opposing

oppressor
outrageous
pale
pangs
puzzles
rub
scorns
shocks
sicklied
spurns
suffer
sweat
troubles
unworthy
weary
wrong

Hesitation, Error, Uncertainty

awry
but
cowards
delay
dread
no
not
pause
perchance
puzzles
questions
something
undiscover'd
unworthy
whether

would
wrong

The Body

ache (from **heart-
ache**)
arms (metonymy for
weapons)
bare (for **bodkin**)
flesh
grunt
heart (from **heart-
ache**)
hue
mortal
pale
sicklied
sweat
weary

Death and Endings

after
consummation
death
die
end
heir
lose
mortal
pale
sleep

Thought

conscience
dream
know
mind
puzzles
question
regard
resolution

respect
thought
wish

The Law, Debate, and Office

heir
law
office
question
quietus
regard
resolution
respect

Weapons

arms
arrows
bodkin
scorns
slings
whips

These categories, again, could be defined differently. And certain words within each of these groupings belong to one or more of the other groupings. But they help us get at some of the most important themes in the soliloquy, including its emphasis on **death**, the **troubles** of **long life** and the interrelation of thought and hesitation, error, and uncertainty. The predominance of words related to **troubles** suggests this idea lies at the center of the speech's concerns.

Words remain the building blocks of the soliloquy. But how Hamlet arranges them deserves our full attention. We have already observed his preference for balancing elements, a balance that often leads to a third thing that does not quite represent the pair it seems to summarize. We have seen his tendency to use duplicated phrases, such as **slings and arrows** and **whips and scorns**. We have also looked at the walking imagery that gradually creeps into the speech, almost desperately turning into the verb **fly** toward the end of his soliloquy. To these features we could add Hamlet's use of explicit metaphors like **sea of troubles** and **sleep of death**, metaphors in which he plainly combines one item (the **sea**, **sleep**) with another (**troubles**, **death**) to produce a third thing that asks us to look at each of its elements anew even as it makes an argument about them. 'One's troubles can be so daunting that they are like the sea.' Where another speaker might have compared these **troubles** to the sands of a beach (in that they seem innumerable), Hamlet perhaps recalls anecdotes about classical figures whose insanity led them to advance on the ocean with drawn swords. We may find a hint of personification in the phrase **outrageous fortune**, the figure of Fortune wielding **slings and arrows**. This may operate as well as in the parallel **whips and scorns of time**, in which we could imagine a personified Time flailing away at us through agents that Hamlet goes on to catalogue: an **oppressor**, a **proud man**, a diffident **love**[r], and so forth.

This **weary life** is like a journey, Hamlet suggests with his metaphors, in which we **bear** the heavy pack of misery. We could choose to **end** this journey ourselves, he continues, were **death** not like traveling to an **undiscover'd country** from which no one has ever returned. Our natural or **native** capacity to resolve upon action is made sick by too much **thought**. And to the extent that great plans are like onrushing rivers, **conscience** induces them to turn away from their proper goal.

Even in this last summary, we sense the power of a heroic mode of expression in the soliloquy. This mode asserts itself through the imagery of weapons, of course: the **slings and arrows**, **arms**, **whips and scorns**, and the **bare bodkin**. It also finds itself strengthened by some of the less apparently martial terms in the speech, by such words as **coil**, **calamity**, and even the notion of far-flung exploration coming from **undiscover'd country**. This register becomes strongest toward the end of the speech. Hamlet seems most commanding, in fact, when he begins the last section of the soliloquy: **Thus conscience does make cowards of us all**. Hamlet's pale-faced resolution – like someone whose visage is **sicklied o'er** with **thought** – anticipates Macbeth's angry words to a servant near the end of his play. The Scottish tyrant returns again and again to the image of fear making the servant pale: 'thou cream-fac'd loon,' he begins, 'Go prick thy face, and over-red thy fear ... those linen cheeks of thine / Are counselors to fear ... whey-face' (*Macbeth* 5.3.11–17). Like Macbeth, who has earlier meditated on the ends of action with a soliloquy on 'the be-all' rather than 'To be or not to be' (1.7.5), Hamlet ends his speech sounding like an angry military officer. Unlike Macbeth, however, the **coward** he criticizes is not a nameless servant but himself – and, by extension, **us all**.

When we replace **nobler** in Hamlet's second line with the less specific 'better' (as in the last chapter's paraphrase), we lose the important sense of distinction and hierarchy that weaves itself throughout his speech. Distinction occupies Hamlet's mind when he catalogues the wrongs we often undergo in life at the hands, for instance, of an **oppressor**, a **proud man**, or a scornful **love**[r]. But it works most strongly in the soliloquy's final section, where distinction is not only implied by such terms as **coward**, but also stated powerfully by the epic phrase **enterprises of great pitch and moment**. This epic strain finds itself resolved in the image of rivers turning their **currents** aside, and in the emphatic final word of the soliloquy proper, **action**.

But the **name of action** is of course lost. The soliloquy as a whole often works through negation, through things that are not, or are taken away. We saw many terms connected with such negation in the list of TROUBLE words given above. Even this list, though, fails to do justice to the speech's reliance on negatives. We think immediately of the famous negation in the initial line – **not to be** – as well as such phrases as **no more, But, no traveller, know not of**, and the idea of negation built into such words as **opposing, end them, die, shuffled off, oppressor's, quietus,** and **lose**. Added to this are prefixes like *un***worthy** and *un***discover'd**. We even have echoes of this negation, of course, in the **no** sound in *no***bler**, and *know* **not**. Each of these last instances comes in the close context of more apparent negations (**not to be, not of**) to produce what we could call a cluster of denial. The last chapter described **quietus** as a loose anagram of Hamlet's more famous **question** minus the letters **n** and **o**. If *m . . . k* is the secret or signature sound of this famous speech, its key word is clearly **no**.

The most important **no** of the soliloquy is hidden in plain sight, concealed in the implied answers to his rhetorical questions: **For who would bear . . .** and **who would fardels bear . . .?** The answer to these questions is of course 'No one.' If Hamlet, internalizing his two angels, utters an 'everyman' soliloquy whose truths pertain to **us all**, the negation at its heart transforms it into a pendulum-like speech about 'no one.' In Hamlet's eyes no one has the courage **not to be** before one's time because no one living knows, by definition, what it is like to be dead. A simple truth, it is for Hamlet what defines our humanity and makes our common life a journey in which we **grunt and sweat** each **weary** step toward **the undiscover'd country** of **death**.

With this 'end' of Hamlet's journey, we are approaching the end of our own examination of how his speech works. It seems the right time, then, both to summarize a few of the things we have observed about the speech and to return to some of the questions we asked about it in this study's second chapter.

To gather our answers to this chapter's central question 'How does this soliloquy work?', we could contrast it with how other soliloquies work. Soliloquies often draw on conventional literary and rhetorical forms, and can thus work like logical arguments, complaints, meditations, prayers, or satires, to name only these. Many soliloquies in Shakespeare and in the plays of his contemporaries reason through particular problems or issues. As we have seen, they sometimes indicate their conclusions or resolutions (or lack thereof) by means of a capping couplet – two rhyming lines such as 'The play's the thing / Wherein I'll catch the conscience of the King!' That we have no such conclusion in the 'To be or not to be' soliloquy does not mean that Hamlet has not come to a conclusion. In his **Thus . . . thus** ending we seem to get a conclusion regarding the shared cowardice that derives from the **conscience** of introspection.

Yet the soliloquy's refusal to give us a conventional, gift-wrapped ending is surely emblematic of a larger truth about how this speech means. Hamlet continually gives and takes away, starting down one path only to reverse directions. Eventually we feel that, while not quite traveling in circles, we are seeing landmarks for the second and even third time as we go over increasingly familiar terrain. At the same time, seeing these landmarks again and again means that they are *un*familiar, even uncanny. We hear its words and know that we have heard them before, but the fact that they mean something else now takes away the purchase they may have with us. Reading, hearing, and speaking this soliloquy is like opening the same door repeatedly, only to discover unaccountably different things behind it each time. Other analogies touch on this sense of surprise. The speech sometimes seems to undulate, like a snake; at other times, the back-and-forth quality of rallies in a tennis match seems the best analogy. If the 'To be or not to be' soliloquy is like a tennis match, we need to see that every now and then a shot is hit not where we expect it, but to an adjoining court – whereupon the point does not end but continues anew.

In its hypnotic back-and-forth motion we may locate one of the secrets of the soliloquy, as well as answers to some of the questions that we asked about this speech earlier. Actors have found this speech difficult for a number of reasons. One of the reasons is its celebrity: Hamlet's soliloquy has been spoken so many times, by so many actors, that 'owning' it onstage is nearly impossible. In truth, it cannot be owned, only rented.

But it is problematic for actors for other reasons as well. Actors are often unhappy about giving this speech because it has been detached from *Hamlet* so often that it has become both monument and cliché. Richard Burton, who played Hamlet in several productions, saw the soliloquy as hopelessly familiar:

> Has there ever been a more boring speech, after 400 years of constant repetition, than 'To be or not to be'? I have never played that particular speech, and I've played the part hundreds and hundreds of times, without knowing that everybody settles down to a nice old nap the minute the first fatal words start.

For Ben Kingsley, the 'fatal words' had a more horrifying effect. Kingsley speaks for many actors when recalling, of his 1975 turn as Hamlet, that the 'To be or not to be' soliloquy produced a 'wave of terror' in him: 'the whole event, the audience out there, knowing you have the most famous soliloquy in the world to do.'

Thus an answer to our question, 'Why have so many actors sought to play Hamlet only to struggle with this speech?' helps solve our second puzzle: 'How could the most famous speech in literature be so mysterious, and so poorly understood?' Its monumental status can make it seem either comic (too familiar to look at) or tragic (too painful to revisit). The undulating movement of this soliloquy – its emphasis on repetition, pairing, and negation – also contributes to a hypnotic and disorienting effect. Like audience members and readers, actors can struggle with a speech that swings back and forth like a hypnotist's gold watch. Sometimes we break this recursive pattern, but even the heroic language of its conclusion builds to an anti-climax. Though a key last word is **action**, it is action, Hamlet tells us, that we have lost in name and deed alike.

This speech's mystery has other sources. A large part of its mystery comes from its concern with the great unknown of all our lives: our inability to know **what dreams may come** in our **sleep of death**; the unspecific **dread** we have **of something after death**; the nature of the **undiscover'd country**. This part of being human **puzzles the will**, Hamlet tells us. If Plato's fable of the Cave has us living ignorantly save for what we can tell of the shadows cast before us (the shadows of we know not whom or what standing behind us), Hamlet's soliloquy insists that we are more ignorant still. We may or may not have dreams after we die; if we do, these dreams may or may not be our afterlife. If they come at all, they may be nightmares. We see no shadows in Hamlet's soliloquy. Even these would be a comfort, for they would indicate something or someone to share our emptiness with. Instead, we are afraid – have **dread** – of what may come as **dreams**. More dreadful than shadows is nothing. Hamlet's speech is mysterious, then, in large part because of its concern with life's mysteries. This concern and these mysteries reverberate through the speech. If Hamlet is agnostic about the afterlife, this lack of knowledge brings him no comfort.

Hamlet's great speech – perhaps the central speech of Western literature – succeeds by denying greatness, by testifying to the unattractive truth that we have survived as human beings by being unable or unwilling to transcend our fears. Life is uncertain and **weary** in Hamlet's account. What his soliloquy manages to convey in its alternately somber and frenetic insights is the repetitive nature of this weariness. This 'high' register speech, so celebrated for its profundity, succeeds by advancing its gray and chilling knowledge through the simple vocabulary that defines our existence: **be**, **suffer**, **die**, **sleep**, **dream**, **lose**. In these words we recognize Hamlet's understanding of this morality play of our life.

To be or not to be

To be, or not to be, that is the question: 55
Whether 'tis nobler in the mind to suffer
The slings and arrows of outrageous fortune,
Or to take arms against a sea of troubles,
And by opposing, end them. To die, to sleep –
No more, and by a sleep to say we end   60
The heart-ache and the thousand natural shocks
That flesh is heir to; 'tis a consummation
Devoutly to be wish'd. To die, to sleep –
To sleep, perchance to dream – ay, there's the rub,
For in that sleep of death what dreams may come,   65
When we have shuffled off this mortal coil,
Must give us pause; there's the respect
That makes calamity of so long life:
For who would bear the whips and scorns of time,
Th' oppressor's wrong, the proud man's contumely,   70
The pangs of despis'd love, the law's delay,
The insolence of office, and the spurns
That patient merit of th' unworthy takes,
When he himself might his quietus make
With a bare bodkin; who would fardels bear,   75
To grunt and sweat under a weary life,
But that the dread of something after death,
The undiscover'd country, from whose bourn
No traveller returns, puzzles the will,
And makes us rather bear those ills we have,   80
Than fly to others that we know not of?
Thus conscience does make cowards of us all,
And thus the native hue of resolution
Is sicklied o'er with the pale cast of thought,
And enterprises of great pitch and moment   85
With this regard their currents turn awry,
And lose the name of action. – Soft you now,
The fair Ophelia.

5 The Name of Action (The Speech in Context)

So far we have looked mainly at the speech 'itself,' exploring what and how it means by taking up its words, phrases, and structures. Reading the speech closely like this can tell us a great deal about what the 'To be or not to be' soliloquy is, at base. Much more than a frozen conglomeration of words, the speech, as we have seen, has an internal dynamic, a set of motions and counter-motions scripted within its lines. To begin to understand its compelling nature, we looked at the structures that lend the speech its uncanny power.

But the meaning of Hamlet's soliloquy depends on more than its words. *Where* the speech is, as well as *from and for whom* it is spoken, has a clear role in its meaning as a dramatic and theatrical utterance. This chapter will focus, then, on some contexts for the speech. We will concern ourselves with three areas in particular: the role of Hamlet's biography in relation to the speech; the place of the speech in the play (including who overhears it); and, finally, reversing this question, the place of the play in the speech.

We could begin by noticing that Hamlet's 'biography' is in his speech, even as his speech is in his biography. The speech and the character define one another. Just as we saw that the speech exists only in and through its words, so does our understanding of Hamlet's character (even our acceptance of him *as* a character) revolve around this speech. Similarly, however often we encounter this speech in advertisements and other cultural venues, it is never fully detachable from Hamlet. Nor can it be separated, in the end, from our recognition of Hamlet's sway upon our shared culture itself.

How can one talk about the biography of a character in a play? Very carefully, clearly, for the word 'biography' presupposes a life substantial enough to have a story that can be told. And Shakespeare's characters are no more and no less than dried ink, figures in scripts that, while often exceeding the 'two hours' traffic' of an afternoon's performance, do not stretch much further than that. The detail we find about characters in many novels is simply not a part of drama from this era. At the same time, though, these plays can give us the feeling that we know a great deal about the characters they present, allowing us to imagine 'back stories' to the actions we see as well as sequels or dramatic afterlives.

That said, the facts of Hamlet's biography would scarcely fill a paragraph. And some of these seem contradictory. Different parts of the play, for instance, imply a different age for him. This ambiguity seems more the rule than the exception where Hamlet is concerned. Indeed, a newspaper obituary could be expected to be quite brief:

> *Prince of Denmark; scholar. Born to the Danish King of the same name, and Queen Gertrude. Upon his father's untimely death, interrupted study at Wittenberg before witnessing Gertrude's marriage to his uncle, Claudius, which complicated his own access to the throne. Alternately melancholy, jocular, sincere, disrespectful, murderous, and stoic, Hamlet died in the infamous palace massacre at Elsinore. He is survived by his close friend and classmate Horatio.*

Clearly Hamlet is many things, and various characters in the play perceive him differently at different moments. He is interesting in part because so much is kept back from us.

Ophelia gives us a list of his multiple roles – real, potential, and imagined – when she characterizes him after his wild 'Get thee to a nunn'ry' behavior. This violent sequence comes, of course, just after he has broken off his 'To be or not to be' soliloquy to acknowledge her entrance. Her familiar catalog laments his decline into what seems insanity:

> O, what a noble mind is here o'erthrown!
> The courtier's, soldier's, scholar's, eye, tongue, sword,
> Th' expectation and rose of the fair state,
> The glass of fashion and the mould of form,
> Th' observ'd of all observers, quite, quite down!

> (3.1.150–4)

We may hear in her 'noble mind' an echo of Hamlet's own **nobler in the mind**. Ophelia has watched Hamlet lose his 'noble and most sovereign reason' and has witnessed his 'unmatch'd form and stature of blown youth / Blasted with ecstasy' (3.1.150–60).

Along with 'reason,' the most important part of her capsule biography may be the word 'scholar's,' which, in Ophelia's rendering, can be understood to join with 'eye.' This line, significantly, jumbles its roles and qualities: we expect 'courtier's . . . tongue,' 'scholar's . . . eye,' and 'soldier's . . . sword,' as this is a conventional set of attributes for the respective roles. But Ophelia re-orders the objects so that no logical pattern underlies their relation to presumably corresponding roles. In another play and another scene this re-ordering could cause more uncertainty than it does here. Ophelia is only following the ecology of the play, however, in disordering the description of a disordered mind – Hamlet's. For Ophelia to follow '1, 2, 3' (the order of the agents: courtier, scholar, soldier) with neither '1, 2, 3' (the order of their attributes or faculties) nor '3, 2, 1' (a perfect inversion) but '3, 1, 2' (a puzzling disorder) is to engage in the very repetition-with-a-difference that we have seen Hamlet himself use in his soliloquy. It is as though in this line Ophelia reveals that she has been infected by Hamlet's penchant for setting up a pattern only to defy our expectations.

Whatever its disorienting dynamics, Hamlet's speech is clearly structured by his scholarly background. A kind of formal disputation, the soliloquy points at the schoolroom where, as we have seen, students were commonly asked to debate one or both sides of a 'question.' One of the foundational problems of all philosophy has been the nature of our existence. As we have noted, the question of 'being or not being' was almost clichéd in the philosophical and logical traditions of both Greece (*on kai me on*) and Rome (*est aut non est*).

But the soliloquy can be seen as coming from more than a generalized schoolroom. Hamlet, we are told, studies at Wittenberg. During Shakespeare's lifetime, the university at Wittenberg was known for producing free thinkers, individuals who were not reluctant to struggle against the received opinions of their day, or to call into question the very premises upon which others lived their lives. Many in Shakespeare's audiences would have associated two notorious free thinkers with Wittenberg: Doctor Faustus and Martin Luther. Each of these figures called orthodoxy into question, with momentous results. Those English subjects familiar with Christopher Marlowe's play *Doctor Faustus*, for instance, would remember that the Wittenberg scholar had learned so much through study and teaching that he was dissatisfied with the sum total of knowledge available to human beings. Selling his soul to the devil, Faustus gained the whole world only to watch his contract come due while he was still unsatisfied. Martin Luther, to anyone valuing religious and political stability, forged a similarly dangerous challenge to authority with his equally radical inquiry. Almost single-handedly ushering in the Reformation – arguably the greatest revolution in Western history – Luther was notorious for casting off the bonds of conventional thinking.

For Shakespeare to identify Hamlet's and Horatio's university as Wittenberg is to give them a home in a European hub of radical thought. As we have seen, conventional academic questions could encompass fairly esoteric matters: for instance, whether one should sow one's wild oats while young, or whether there are other worlds than this one. Hamlet's **question**, instead, goes to the very heart of our life, raising issues of existence, agency, and the afterlife. The playwright appropriately credited Wittenberg, the spiritual nursery of these two figures, with producing their intellectual cousin, Prince Hamlet. 'To be or not to be,' then, is a student's speech, and the speech of a student who has been encouraged to think in radical ways.

Hamlet himself speaks of his 'inky cloak' and his 'customary suits of solemn black' (1.2.77–8), and the black garb that has long since been the costume of bohemians remains something like an identifying badge for his melancholy. Indeed, in addition to his status as a student, Hamlet's melancholy often plays a role in how his actions and words are interpreted. In an interview given about portraying Hamlet in his film version of the play, for instance, Mel Gibson related that he based his performance in part on what he learned about the character by looking up the word 'melancholy' in a dictionary. What he found there – definitions centering on such words as 'sad' and 'gloomy' – is not necessarily untrue to the shapes of Hamlet's personality in the play. There are moments when these terms perfectly describe Hamlet's actions and words. Perhaps 'melancholy' even describes Hamlet's state of mind during the soliloquy.

But 'melancholy' meant more than merely 'sad' for the Elizabethans; it encompassed a broad pattern of behavior that included bursts of utter creativity and genius. One of the pseudo-Aristotelian philosophical 'problems' that students were asked to wrestle with in their debates, in fact, concerned why it is that all great thinkers, artists, generals, and political leaders have been melancholy in nature. That is, while a 'melancholy' person may strike modern-day culture as a depressive in need of medication, Shakespeare's age was ready to recognize a melancholic as possessing one of the pre-conditions of genius. The sub-culture of academic Humanism, in fact, nurtured the cult of melancholy in part by encouraging meditations on one's mortality. Skulls – like the one Hamlet will speak to in his famous encounter with the Gravediggers (5.1) – became something like a token of one's intellectual seriousness. They were reminders of death's presence in our lives: *memento mori*. Together with his inky cloak, melancholy, and address to Yorick's skull, Hamlet's 'To be or not to be' soliloquy marks him as a figure of the radical, doubting, even malcontented intellectual of post-Reformation Europe.

If Hamlet's 'biography' informs his speech in this way, the soliloquy also completes his biography. Our picture of Hamlet usually involves him either holding a skull or speaking this speech. Frequently, advertisements and other parodies have him doing both simultaneously. Why has this soliloquy come to serve as an essential part of his biography? And in what way does this soliloquy complete, or at least add to, our understanding of his dramatic life? First of all, it stands as a metaphor of what we see throughout the play: Hamlet often keeps his words to himself. His first line in the play, as set in most editions, is an aside: 'A little more than kin, and less than kind' (1.2.65). And, as we have noticed, the 'To be or not to be' soliloquy is one of a half-dozen soliloquies he speaks in *Hamlet*. If we needed a better example of Hamlet's intellectual, spiritual, and social solitude, Shakespeare would have been hard pressed to provide it.

But this soliloquy is particularly good at showing something for which Hamlet is notorious: his indecision. Laurence Olivier's film version of *Hamlet* summarizes a common understanding of Hamlet's character by intoning, at its opening: 'This is the tragedy of a man who could not make up his mind.' As a reading of either *Hamlet* or Hamlet, such leaves a little bit to be desired. Yet Olivier's sentence accurately characterizes one line of thinking about the play and its central figure: Hamlet is an indecisive intellectual, a man who knows too much, who is paralyzed by the weight and results of thought. In this interpretation, thinking is not only a mode of life that Hamlet embraces, but forms an unhealthy addiction. It would be much better (this interpretation tends to suggest) if Hamlet were to act as Othello acts, killing Claudius at some moment in Act 3 and sending everyone home early. In this reading, the soliloquy stands as a capsule summary of what remains wrong with Hamlet: he cannot bring himself to do what he needs to do because he is thinking about doing rather than doing. He substitutes, for the action of his body, the action of his mind.

As we have seen, though, the speech has more than thought in it. Or rather, Hamlet makes thought a kind of action. The heroic register the soliloquy builds up to – **enterprises of great pitch and moment** – is not only rousing in itself but gives us reason to think that Hamlet has action within him. As Ophelia's catalog suggests, Hamlet is part soldier in this play, that itself begins and ends with soldiers. We see him willing to act at various moments in the play, and he draws his sword on a number of occasions before dueling with Laertes and killing the King at the play's climax. We will return to the way this soliloquy captures larger elements of the play within it, but for now it is important to acknowledge that it focuses on more than indecision. In its gradually escalating language of action, it doubles the trajectory that Hamlet himself will follow in the play.

Action, indecision, melancholy, solitude: these are a few of the things that the speech represents for Hamlet's character. But it is not safe to assume that the speech means only privately, for and about Hamlet. That is, while we have called this speech a soliloquy throughout this book, a number of critics (and certain theatrical productions) have suggested that Hamlet's speech is less private than is widely believed. To the biographical context, then, we need to add a theatrical and dramatic one. This context may help us address an important question: Who hears Hamlet's speech, and how do we know what they hear?

Obviously *we* hear the speech, regardless of whether Hamlet delivers it, in the theater, directly to us, speaks it to himself, or combines these two modes – sharing certain words, phrases, or sentences with us, that is, but speaking others to himself, as though in dialogue with what Philip Sidney calls one's 'inward guest.' In a basic sense, then, Hamlet *is* overheard as he delivers this soliloquy. But do any of his fellow characters in the world of *Hamlet* overhear him? This is a more troubling question than is sometimes acknowledged, for while we understand soliloquies to be moments of private speech and thought, the court of Elsinore in *Hamlet* is a place of almost constant surveillance: almost without exception, the play's major characters watch each other in hope of gaining information that can be employed for advantage. And as Claudius remarks prior to Hamlet's speech,

> we have closely sent for Hamlet hither,
> That he, as 'twere by accident, may here
> Affront Ophelia. Her father and myself,
> We'll so bestow ourselves that, seeing unseen,
> We may of their encounter frankly judge,
> And gather by him, as he is behav'd,
> If 't be th' affliction of his love or no
> That thus he suffers for.

(3.1.29–36)

Clearly the King intends this to be a kind of 'mousetrap' for Hamlet. His fellow voyeur, Polonius, cannot guess Claudius's real reason for wanting to know the source of Hamlet's 'suffer[ing].' And although these men have presumably 'bestow[ed]' themselves somewhere close to the place Hamlet delivers his soliloquy, it seems unlikely that an audience would see them during the speech itself, or that we would benefit from such a spectacle.

Basing their understanding of this scene on the King's intent to 'frankly judge' Hamlet's and Ophelia's 'encounter,' some critics have held that we must take their spying into account when we read and hear the 'To be or not to be' speech. Others venture further, suggesting that this spying does not go unnoticed by Hamlet himself. In fact there are a number of ways to read the speech in relation to its immediate dramatic context. Here are a few:

1. Hamlet is not overheard as he speaks.
2. Hamlet is overheard as he speaks, but is unaware that he is overheard.
3. Hamlet is overheard as he speaks, and is aware the entire time that he is overheard.
4. Hamlet is overheard as he speaks, and becomes aware during the speech that he is being overheard.

Of these four, again, no. 1 seems supported by much of what surrounds the speech. Claudius, we will recall, states that they will judge 'seeing unseen,' a phrase that we could take to suggest that they will hide and watch from some distance (most likely offstage) – presumably checking to see if Hamlet acts the way jilted lovers typically act.

But there is more to the scene than that. After the loud 'nunn'ry' exchange, the King and Polonius enter and both claim that they have heard what Hamlet has uttered. 'You need not tell us what Lord Hamlet said,' Polonius tells Ophelia, 'We heard it all' (3.1.179–80). Claudius speaks of this at more length:

> Love? his affections do not that way tend,
> Nor what he spake, though it lack'd form a little,
> Was not like madness. There's something in his soul
> O'er which his melancholy sits on brood,
> And I do doubt the hatch and the disclose
> Will be some danger ...

> (3.1.162–7)

It is not clear whether we are supposed to believe that Claudius and Polonius have heard everything that Hamlet has said after they hide themselves, or whether the 'To be or not to be' speech has been largely private, with Hamlet's remarks in prose to Ophelia forming the bulk of what the older men overhear. Readers and actors sometimes fasten upon Hamlet's unprompted question to Ophelia – 'Where's your father?' (129) – as indicating a sudden awareness, on Hamlet's part, that he is being watched. This 'aware' Hamlet then turns his angry remarks toward the pair's hiding place as he threatens 'I say we will have no moe marriage. Those that are married already (all but one) shall live, the rest shall keep as they are' (147–9).

It is just as unclear what the interpretations that see Hamlet as not only overheard but conscious of being overheard would mean for the structure and delivery of the soliloquy. One can, of course, take the heroic register in the speech's final lines as an anticipation of the blustery language Hamlet will deliver in his 'no moe marriage' lines. But his diction in 'To be or not to be' is really so generalized that it is difficult to imagine Claudius understanding the speech as a personal threat to his, Claudius's, hold on power. Of course, Claudius's characterization of Hamlet following the nunnery exchange is also a good description of Hamlet's state as he delivers his soliloquy: 'There's something in his soul / O'er which his melancholy sits on brood' (164–5). The arresting image Claudius gives us of Hamlet is one in which an unidentified 'something' resides, egg-like, in Hamlet's 'soul;' on this egg Hamlet's 'melancholy' sits, like a hen, waiting for it (even as it helps it) to hatch.

The King's eventual solution to the problem of Hamlet is to send Hamlet to England with a sealed letter instructing the English monarch to execute him. It seems unlikely that all this certainty comes from the 'To be or not to be' speech, which, while it testifies to the prince's melancholy, seems a less specific spur to Claudius than the 'no moe marriage' comment. If Hamlet is clearly shown to be overheard, and if he likewise clearly realizes he is overheard, this probably happens after, rather than during, his famous soliloquy. The presence of a perceived audience onstage would change our sense (as well as Hamlet's) of the direction and function of his words, adding yet other layers of potential manipulation to the speech. It may be permissible to think that the soliloquy has enough thought in and around it – prompts so much thinking and interpretation on its own – that we are allowed, with Hamlet, momentarily to forget that he may be overheard at his most intimate moment.

If we temporarily lose track of the play around Hamlet's speech, we should not miss the way in which *Hamlet* itself is in this soliloquy. We have already seen that so much of Hamlet's 'biography' seems to be in his speech. There is another sense in which we can take *Hamlet*, the play, to be in the soliloquy – a presence that is as great as if not greater than the unfolding of the prince's biography in it. Almost every important structuring device in *Hamlet*, from the level of characterization through thought, language, and action itself, is present in the 'To be or not to be' soliloquy. In this way, Hamlet's famous speech works as something like a miniature version of the play itself. As the Prince himself might put it, 'To be or not to be' is *Hamlet* 'bounded in a nutshell' (2.2.254).

We can perceive how the soliloquy incorporates these external structures by examining, in quick sequence, some of the parts that we discerned in the last chapter. Take, for instance, the way in which opposition structures the first part of the soliloquy:

> To be, or not to be, that is the question:
> Whether 'tis nobler in the mind to suffer
> The slings and arrows of outrageous fortune,
> Or to take arms against a sea of troubles,
> And by opposing, end them.

This passage does many things. One of the things it does most clearly is foreground conflict and opposition. From its initial opposition of **To be** with **not to be**, and its balanced alternatives (**Whether ... Or**), to its concluding use of the word **opposing**, the first four-and-a-half lines of Hamlet's 'To be or not to be' soliloquy structure his options in terms of conflicting, binary divisions. Hamlet can either **take arms** against his **troubles** or continue to have such **arms** – figured as **slings and arrows** – used against him.

All drama centers on conflict. But as a revenge tragedy, *Hamlet* seems especially full of the oppositions and conflicting pairs that we see in this speech's opening section. Putting aside Hamlet's own motive for revenge, we notice that the international conflict in the play's 'overplot' (a structural division between states, cities, institutions, or families) sets Denmark in direct opposition to Norway. Horatio tells us that, 'prick'd on by a most emulate pride,' old Fortinbras challenged Hamlet's father to single combat; his defeat in that conflict has led his son, young Fortinbras, to seek to regain the lands his father's risky duel has cost him (1.1.83). For its part, Laertes' grudge against Hamlet will close the play by surfacing in what Osric will dub 'the opposition of your person in trial' (5.2.171–2). The kind of stark 'opposition' characterizing these duels finds embodiment not only in the soliloquy's central distinction between **thought** and **action**, but in nearly every one of the play's scenes. We could think of the way Hamlet hectors Gertrude to 'Look here upon this picture, and on this, / The counterfeit presentment of two brothers' (3.4.53–4), a moment when productions have typically offered physical representations (portraits, miniatures) to set out the differences between what Hamlet feels to be absolutely different brothers. Likewise another of the drama's use of stage properties, Hamlet's celebrated address of Yorick's skull, puts into play the stark differences between the past and the present, the living and the dead.

We could multiply instances of opposition, for it is not only classic cinema that gives us black-and-white memories of the play. Throughout, Shakespeare's tragedy relies on vivid instances of contrast. These instances are gathered – and many of them are summarized – by the balanced oppositions of the beginning of Hamlet's 'To be or not to be' soliloquy.

But, as any reader of *Hamlet* also knows, the play tends to collapse such oppositions almost as soon as they are constructed. The wonderfully complex beginning of the play, for instance, creates an initial opposition of guard and stranger that resolves itself into a fearful conversation between comrades and 'rivals.' Likewise the appearance of the Ghost calls into question any easy opposition between the living and the dead (even as it effectively nullifies, of course, the truth of Hamlet's remark about the **undiscover'd country, from whose bourn no traveller returns**). The dividing line between the quick and the dead becomes blurred, too, when Yorick's skull mocks Hamlet with death's role in our every move, with the inescapable presence of the skull beneath our skin. And one point that we may take from Hamlet's blustery encounter with his mother is that, however different he considers old Hamlet and Claudius to be, Gertrude finds it easy to replace brother with brother in her bed.

Along with oppositions in this play, then, we need to consider the function of its intensive pairings and resemblances. *Hamlet* is uncannily concerned with doublings, with pairs and partners, and near twins. We could take the almost inseparable Rosencrantz and Guildenstern as a central example of this tendency, but this duo is only one instance of what we see throughout *Hamlet*. The father–son relationship of old and young Fortinbras is replicated in the Danish pair of old and young Hamlet. The brother–brother pairing of old Hamlet and Claudius finds replication not only in the play-within-the-play's story of regicide, but in the pair of gravediggers and in the relationship of Hamlet and Horatio, whose friendship is nearly the last surviving bond we encounter in the play. This patterning-by-twos is also present with the two men who love Ophelia – Laertes and Hamlet – who of course wrestle in her grave before dueling with foils. If *Hamlet* gives us many stark oppositions, it is also concerned, as a drama, to show us pairings and resemblances, and moments where things that have seemed to be different come to reveal their similarities.

Following the speech's initial emphasis on opposition, the second section of Hamlet's famous soliloquy asks us to think about such resemblance through its use of the conventional 'death as sleep' metaphor:

> To die, to sleep –
> No more, and by a sleep to say we end
> The heart-ache and the thousand natural shocks
> That flesh is heir to; 'tis a consummation
> Devoutly to be wish'd.

We have already examined the kinds of things that the first lines of this section could mean: whether we are to take **No more**, for instance, as a phrase of self-reproach, or whether with it Hamlet is re-stating **To die** (that is, death as a state in which one would be **No more**). Regardless of which option we feel best captures the meaning of these lines, it is clear that they rely on the 'death as sleep' pairing – a pairing that allows us to tell ourselves that a corpse in a coffin looks like it is 'sleeping,' or that we are putting a pet 'to sleep.' The notion of an easeful death briefly comforts Hamlet as he imagines that this will **end** both **heart-ache** and **the thousand natural shocks that flesh is heir to**. The hoped-for partnership of **die** and **sleep** will overcome the established pairing of **flesh** and **shocks**. At the end of the second line here we have the word **end**, followed two lines later of course by **consummation**, which also ends its line. In his thought-experiment, Hamlet seems to be trying out ideas in a quest for certainty about something.

Yet it is in his nature as a character, even as it is in the nature of *Hamlet* as a play, to derive no certainty from either resemblances or oppositions. With Hamlet, as with *Hamlet*, all structures seem to be continually dissolving into something else: we could recall the 'Very like a while' sequence in which Hamlet teases Polonius about inter-preting the shapes of clouds (3.2.376–82). Thus the 'death is sleep' metaphor cannot provide Hamlet with a peaceful or harmonious partnership, any more than the terms of an opposition can remain in tension with one another without revealing their similarities. The next section of his soliloquy stages something we see throughout the drama generally – the inability of settlements to stay settled:

> To die, to sleep –
> To sleep, perchance to dream – ay, there's the rub,
> For in that sleep of death what dreams may come,
> When we have shuffled off this mortal coil,
> Must give us pause; there's the respect
> That makes calamity of so long life:

Hamlet's **rub** functions as a center for this thought. Referring, as we have seen, to the block or impediment in a game of bowls, this word stands in for the insight that has just come to Hamlet: that the 'death as sleep' partnership is not necessarily any more free from trouble or strife than **sleep** is in life. Hamlet fears (at the very least, acknowledges the possibility of) the bad dreams that may characterize any afterlife we have. Even as resemblances throughout the play – of brother to brother, father to son, lover to lover – not only fail to produce peace or harmony, but in fact tend to generate or continue opposition, so does the resemblance of **sleep** to **death** work to produce the **rub** of Hamlet's provisional solution to the famous **question** of his soliloquy.

The word **question** brings us to the next sections of his speech, here combined as 13 lines which contain paired rhetorical questions:

> For who would bear the whips and scorns of time,
> Th' oppressor's wrong, the proud man's contumely,
> The pangs of despis'd love, the law's delay,
> The insolence of office, and the spurns
> That patient merit of th' unworthy takes,
> When he himself might his quietus make
> With a bare bodkin; who would fardels bear,
> To grunt and sweat under a weary life,
> But that the dread of something after death,
> The undiscover'd country, from whose bourn
> No traveller returns, puzzles the will,

And makes us rather bear those ills we have,
Than fly to others that we know not of?

The word **question** in his soliloquy's opening line refers, again, to the topic of an academic debate, but at its root lies the same grammatical form of inquiry that appears in queries about (for instance) the time of day. We have seen that these lines pose rhetorical questions, effectively masking (or not masking, as the case may be) statements: 'No one would bear X, if Y weren't the case.' Yet it means something that Hamlet has begun his soliloquy by announcing a question, and goes on to pose a pair of questions (what the Riverside presents as a single two-part question) in the longest sentence of his speech.

Questions make *Hamlet* into a dramatic mystery, with Hamlet as the play's central detective. We could notice how often he interrogates those around him. '[A]re you honest?' he asks Ophelia in the 'nunn'ry' exchange following his soliloquy, 'Are you fair?' (3.1.102, 104). We perceive something central to Hamlet's character – and to the play that bears his name – when we track his responses to Horatio's stunning news about the Ghost. Like a seasoned interrogator trying to find inconsistencies in a story, Hamlet suspiciously probes Horatio for specific details:

Saw, who?
The King my father?
For God's love let me hear!
But where was this?
Did you not speak to it?
'Tis very strange.
Indeed, indeed, sirs. But this troubles me.
Hold you the watch tonight?
Arm'd, say you?
From top to toe?
Then saw you not his face.
What, look'd he frowningly?

Pale, or red?
And fix'd his eyes upon you?
I would I had been there.
Very like, very like. Stay'd it long?
His beard was grisl'd, no?

(1.2.190–239)

His utterances here, marked by 12 brief but insistent questions, contrast formally with his more leisured soliloquies. His longest sentence
is six words long, and his shortest – 'Saw, who?' – only two.

Yet what this interrogation has in common with not only the
soliloquy but the play as a whole is its emphasis on questioning. Like
its title character, the tragedy is dedicated to inquiry. Hamlet sets out
to solve the mystery of his father's murder, a mystery which will bring
him face-to-face with questions concerning his own identity and
human existence generally. His quest will create a mystery ('Is Hamlet
mad, or feigning madness for a reason?') that others (both inside the
play and out) will try to solve: Rosencrantz and Guildenstern will lose
their lives, as Hamlet puts it, for their attempt to 'pluck out the heart
of [his] mystery' (3.2.365–6). For his part, Polonius treats his son
Laertes' course of study at Paris as a mystery not to be solved but
created; he instructs his spy Reynaldo to spread rumors of Laertes'
potential misdemeanors in hopes of finding corroborating witnesses
to any wrongdoings his son may have committed, or be about to
commit. He characterizes these attempts with a summary that has
since become part of our language: 'And thus do we of wisdom and of
reach, / With windlasses and with assays of bias, / By indirections find
directions out' (2.1.61–3).

The moment when one may 'find directions out' – the end of the
detective narratives we see throughout *Hamlet* – comes when, and
only when, the questioner feels confident in drawing a conclusion.
Such confidence is rarely complete, not only because of Hamlet's

indecision but because there are few straight lines to follow in this play – instances, that is, where characters may freely step from A to B and draw conclusion C without hesitation. Even a ghost coming back from the dead to recount the gory·details of being murdered provides no certainty for his listener. It may be no accident that Polonius's summary includes not only 'windlasses,' which the Riverside defines as 'roundabout methods,' but also the phrase 'with assays of bias,' an image which comes, like **there's the rub**, from the game of bowls. The word 'bias' refers to the unequal weight of a ball and/or the uneven surface of the bowling surface. Polonius's 'assays' probably means both measuring or gauging any uneven distribution of weight or unlevel playing surface and the act of trying to bowl successfully using the imperfections of such a ball or surface to one's advantage. A more accessible image is that of a golfer putting a lopsided ball on a sharply breaking green. The many conclusions in *Hamlet* that characters and readers seek come through, and only through, these kind of 'indirections.'

The final section of Hamlet's soliloquy contains within it versions of these conclusions even as it foregrounds the play's emphasis on consequence and causation:

Thus conscience does make cowards of us all,
And thus the native hue of resolution
Is sicklied o'er with the pale cast of thought,
And enterprises of great pitch and moment
With this regard their currents turn awry,
And lose the name of action. – Soft you now,
The fair Ophelia.

Hamlet's **Thus . . . and thus** savors of the schoolroom, of course, and his soliloquy's grounding in academic debate. But it also signals the play's larger interest in drawing conclusions and seeking out causes. The initial dialogue between the Gravediggers comes close to parodying this emphasis. The first Gravedigger sounds like Hamlet as he says 'I'll put another question to thee,' and throughout uses the chop-logic of stage clowns to solve riddles of legal complexity and social life alike. As he expounds to his fellow worker:

> Here lies the water; good. Here stands the man; good. If the man go to this water and drown himself, it is, will he, nill he, he goes, mark you that. But if the water come to him and drown him, he drowns not himself; argal, he that is not guilty of his own death shortens not his own life.

(5.1.15–20)

Likewise, his question concerning strong builders: 'What is he that builds stonger than either the mason, the shipwright, or the carpenter?' (41–2). It is worth paying attention to the fact that this 'low' character in *Hamlet* seems to revel in his question-posing ability. This may be not only because in posing questions he is doing precisely what Hamlet and so many of the play's other characters do (that is, exercising a certain kind of authority), but also because the goal of his questions is finding answers. His 'argal' is a clown's version of the Latin *ergo* or 'therefore,' and his answer to his own riddle ('say "a grave-maker": the houses he makes lasts till doomsday' [58–9]) is also a conclusion depending on logic.

The **Thus . . . and thus** portion of Hamlet's soliloquy encapsulates the larger drama's tendency to make inferences based on observations, and to draw conclusions from what seems probable. Things are famously 'out of joint' in Denmark. Even the soldiers who begin the play – we will recall the opening line 'Who's there?' – press Horatio to explain what they have noticed not only in the fact that they have been put to 'strict and most observant watch' but also that Denmark seems to be preparing feverishly for war. Marcellus's question, structured 'Why . . . Why' over ten lines (1.1.70–9) can be seen as the same form that Hamlet answers with his **Thus . . . and thus** section. Marcellus's question concerns why so much is being done, why so much seems to be in preparation to do something else. For its part,

Hamlet's answer points to the way such preparations for the heroic always go **awry**.

We could adduce many further examples of correspondence between the sections of the soliloquy, and the larger play of which it is a part. The preceding points, though, may serve to suggest the deep presence of the play in the soliloquy. We have seen that Hamlet's biography is in the speech to an extent that rivals the speech's presence in his biography. And while the soliloquy is in the play the play is also in the soliloquy: 'To be or not to be' succeeds, in fact, by folding within its lines many of the major themes and structures of *Hamlet*. Whether centering on oppositions, resemblances, questions, or conclusions, each of its sections contains within it hints of the modes explored by the speech's other parts. But in featuring a central mode of thought, being, or action represented in the play, each works to ensure that the tragedy of *Hamlet* is not only around the soliloquy, but in it.

To be or not to be

To be, or not to be, that is the question: 55
Whether 'tis nobler in the mind to suffer
The slings and arrows of outrageous fortune,
Or to take arms against a sea of troubles,
And by opposing, end them. To die, to sleep –
No more, and by a sleep to say we end   60
The heart-ache and the thousand natural shocks
That flesh is heir to; 'tis a consummation
Devoutly to be wish'd. To die, to sleep –
To sleep, perchance to dream – ay, there's the rub,
For in that sleep of death what dreams may come,   65
When we have shuffled off this mortal coil,
Must give us pause; there's the respect
That makes calamity of so long life:
For who would bear the whips and scorns of time,
Th' oppressor's wrong, the proud man's contumely,   70
The pangs of despis'd love, the law's delay,
The insolence of office, and the spurns
That patient merit of th' unworthy takes,
When he himself might his quietus make
With a bare bodkin; who would fardels bear,   75
To grunt and sweat under a weary life,
But that the dread of something after death,
The undiscover'd country, from whose bourn
No traveller returns, puzzles the will,
And makes us rather bear those ills we have,   80
Than fly to others that we know not of?
Thus conscience does make cowards of us all,
And thus the native hue of resolution
Is sicklied o'er with the pale cast of thought,
And enterprises of great pitch and moment   85
With this regard their currents turn awry,
And lose the name of action. – Soft you now,
The fair Ophelia.

6 Not One Speech but Three, or 'There's the Point'

Earlier we noticed that more than one version of the 'To be or not to be' soliloquy was published in Shakespeare's lifetime. We remarked that the speech commonly read and acted comes from the second quarto (known in abbreviated form as 'Q2'), published in 1604/5, and the First Folio, published in 1623. While the First Folio was a lavish, costly volume, quartos were fairly inexpensive texts, the paperbacks of their day. The name 'quarto' comes from the number of leaves produced when a sheet of paper was folded to make a book's pages — in this case, four. As we saw, the first text of *Hamlet* we have — that of Q1 or the first quarto of 1603 — may have been an unauthorized publication. Its version of the 'To be or not to be' speech differs drastically from the better-known form examined in the preceding pages.

But even the more favorably received texts have some differences worth noting. In fact, the most familiar version of 'To be or not to be' does not exist in any text from Shakespeare's time. Instead, it has been produced by conflating the Q2 and Folio (F) editions of the play — each of which has certain words and phrases not found in the other. This is true of our text of the speech, which comes from the *Riverside Shakespeare*, 2nd edition. For instance, the *Riverside* declines to adopt Folio's 'dispriz'd Love,' keeping **despis'd love**; likewise it does not accept Folio's 'these fardels bear' for **fardels bear**. It does, however, choose to print **cowards of us all**, where the line in Q2 reads simply 'conscience does make cowards,' and it also keeps Q2's **pitch and moment** instead of adopting Folio's 'pith and moment.' An unintentionally humorous reading in the Folio version of the soliloquy gives 'the poor man's contumely' for what Q2 has as **the proud man's contumely**. It is fair to call this humorous because it is hard to imagine Hamlet, banker-like, including the 'contumely' of the poor in a catalog of life's great ills!

For the most part, the Q2 and Folio 'To be or not to be' have only minor differences. In contrast, the soliloquy published in Q1 *Hamlet* is astoundingly different. It is reproduced here with spelling and punctuation modernized to approximate the edited version of the speech we have examined earlier:

> To be or not to be, Ay, there's the point:
> To die, to sleep — is that all? Ay, all:
> No, to sleep, to dream — Ay, marry, there it goes,
> For in that dream of death, when we awake,
> And borne before an everlasting Judge
> From whence no passenger ever return'd,
> The undiscover'd country, at whose sight
> The happy smile, and the accursed damn'd.
> But for this, the joyful hope of this,
> Who'ld bear the scorns and flattery of the world,
> Scorned by the rich — the rich cursed of the poor?
> The widow being oppressed, the orphan wrong'd,
> The taste of hunger, or a tyrant's reign,
> And thousand more calamities besides,
> To grunt and sweat under this weary life,
> When that he may his full quietus make,
> With a bare bodkin, who would this endure,
> But for a hope of something after death?
> Which puzzles the brain, and doth confound the sense,

> Which makes us rather bear those evils we have,
> Than fly to others that we know not of.
> Ay, that: O, this conscience makes cowards of us all,
> Lady in thy orisons, be all my sins rememb'red.

On the whole, this can seem pretty bad stuff. It seems especially lacking when compared with the more familiar version of the speech. There is good reason that Q1 has been called the 'bad' quarto of *Hamlet*. Like much of the play we know through Q2 and the Folio, this speech is *Hamlet* as though heard under water.

The best scholarship we have suggests that Q1 was constructed from memory by the actor who played Marcellus, using an already truncated and rearranged (for theatrical performance) version of what would become the Folio *Hamlet*. This conclusion is based in part on the fact that the lines the Marcellus-actor speaks in the longer versions of the play, as well as those he would have heard just before and after he entered various scenes, are very close to the way they read in Q2 and F. The longer the Marcellus-actor was away from the action, however, the less Q1's lines have in common with Q2 and F, leading scholars to conclude that Q1 is a 'memorially reconstructed' text: a text, that is, constructed from someone's memory – in this case, that of the actor who originally played Marcellus.

If Q1 is a 'bootleg' version of *Hamlet*, we could unpack the analogy as follows. Imagine a modern-day recording engineer. Having helped record an album, he has heard the songs so many times that he is able to reproduce many of their melodies, chords, and lyrics from memory. On his own, and perhaps at the urging of co-workers, he reconstructs an approximation of it, re-ordering some of the songs and changing others' names. This bootleg version has some of the material from the original version he has worked on, and is delightful in its own way. When compared with the original versions, however, it seems inferior. The mystery about Q1 *Hamlet* is not so much 'how' or even 'when' it was produced, but 'why'? Why would the Marcellus-actor choose, or be asked, to reconstruct the *Hamlet* he had performed in? Perhaps the 1603 outbreak of Plague in London prevented the players from having access to their playhouse's books. Perhaps Q1 was the product of a rogue player or group of players who felt this was a good way to turn a profit, however meager. We may never have a good answer to this question. For more information on this fascinating topic, the reader is urged to consult the anthology on Q1 mentioned in the Further Reading section at this end of this book.

But should we be satisfied merely to call this speech (and Q1 generally) 'bad'? Probably not, for even if we accept scholarship's theory of how Q1 and its 'There's the point' soliloquy came to be, we can learn from the speech. To begin with, it is not every day that we get an Elizabethan actor writing down what he remembers of performing Shakespeare's most famous play. So even though the version of the speech he constructed is inferior to the speech we know (perhaps *because* it is inferior in certain ways), it can tell us what the more familiar 'To be or not to be' soliloquy is by showing us some of the things it is not. Some of the ways, that is, in which Shakespeare *could* have written the soliloquy but seems not to have.

Second, the 'There's the point' soliloquy can highlight various things that appear to have struck the Marcellus-actor as being important: key words, phrases, and ideas. Imagine, for instance, that you were asked to reconstruct Hamlet's soliloquy, or another important passage in Shakespeare's works. What mixture of Shakespearean and non-Shakespearean phrases would you produce? Would you be able to reconstruct Macbeth's 'Tomorrow, and tomorrow' soliloquy (*Macbeth* 5.5.19–28)? Many of us would handle the first line adequately, and could even finish strongly with 'It is a tale / Told by an idiot, full of sound and fury, / Signifying nothing.' But what about the material between its beginning and end? If we recalled the lines 'a poor player, / That struts and frets his hour upon the stage,' would we likewise remember 'Life's but a walking shadow' and 'And then is heard no more'? What about the other words and phrases? The version of Macbeth's speech we would produce, like the version of Hamlet's soliloquy reconstructed by an Elizabethan actor, would probably diverge from Shakespeare's better-known words. But what we did remember could well tell others what we found important or otherwise memorable about the speech.

So just *how* the Q1 speech turns awry is significant. Therefore let us examine two versions of the 'To be or not to be' speech side-by-side. We will begin with the received version based on Q2 and Folio *Hamlet*. It is the soliloquy reproduced and studied in the preceding pages. In the reproduction here, the material that Q1 did *not* take up is italicized. The words and phrases shared by the traditional version and the Q1 version are bolded in both versions of the speech. Following the traditional version of the soliloquy is the Q1 version. So that readers can better discern its original material, words and phrases unique to it have there been underlined.

Traditional Version; material shared with Q1 bolded

> **To be or not to be,** *that i*s **the** *question:*
> *Whether 'tis nobler in the mind to suffer*
> *The slings and arrows of outrageous fortune,*
> *Or to take arms against a sea of troubles,*
> *And by opposing, end them.* **To die, to sleep –**
> **No** *more, and by a sleep to say we end*
> *The heart-ache and the thousand natural shocks*
> *That flesh is heir to; 'tis a consummation*
> *Devoutly to be wish'd. To die, to sleep –*
> **To sleep,** *perchance* **to dream – ay, there***'s the rub,*
> **For in that** *sleep* **of death** *what dreams may come,*
> **When we** *have shuffled off this mortal coil,*
> *Must give us pause; there's the respect*

That makes **calamity** *of so long life:*
For **who would bear the whips and scorns of time,**
Th' **oppressor's wrong** *the proud man's contumely,*
The pangs of despis'd love, the law's delay,
The insolence of office, and the spurns
That patient merit of th' unworthy takes,
When he *himself might* **his quietus make**
With a bare bodkin; who would *fardels bear,*
To grunt and sweat under *a* **weary life,**
But *that the dread* **of something after death,**
The undiscover'd country, from *whose* **bourn**
No *traveller* **return***s,* **puzzles the** *will,*
And **makes us rather bear those ills we have,**
Than fly to others that we know not of?
Thus conscience *does* **make cowards of us all,**
And thus the native hue of resolution
Is sicklied o'er with the pale cast of thought,
And enterprises of great pitch and moment
With this regard their currents turn awry,
And lose the name of action. – Soft you now,
The fair Ophelia. Nymph, **in thy orisons**
Be all my sins rememb'red.

Q1 Version; shared material bolded, new material underlined

To be or not to be, <u>Ay, there</u>**'s the** <u>point:</u>
To die, to sleep – <u>is that all? Ay, all:</u>
No, to sleep, to dream – **Ay,** <u>marry,</u> **there** <u>it goes,</u>
For in that <u>dream</u> **of death**, **when** <u>we awake,</u>
<u>And</u> **borne** <u>before an everlasting Judge</u>
From <u>whence</u> **no** <u>passenger</u> <u>ever</u> **return**'d,

> **The undiscover'd country**, <u>at whose sight</u>
> <u>The happy smile, and the accursed damn'd.</u>
> <u>But for this, the joyful hope of this,</u>
> **Who'ld bear the scorns and** <u>flattery</u> **of** <u>the world,</u>
> <u>Scorned by the rich — the rich, cursed of the poor?</u>
> <u>The widow being</u> **oppress**<u>ed, the orphan</u> **wrong**'<u>d,</u>
> <u>The taste of hunger, or a tyrant's reign,</u>
> <u>And thousand more</u> **calamiti**<u>es besides,</u>
> **To grunt and sweat under** <u>this</u> **weary life,**
> **When** <u>that</u> **he** <u>may</u> **his** <u>full</u> **quietus make,**
> **With a bare bodkin, who would** <u>this endure,</u>
> **But** <u>for a hope</u> **of something after death?**
> <u>Which</u> **puzzles the** <u>brain, and doth confound the sense,</u>
> <u>Which</u> **makes us rather bear those** <u>ev</u>**ils we have,**
> **Than fly to others that we know not of.**
> <u>Ay, that: O,</u> **this conscience make**<u>s</u> **cowards of us all,**
> <u>Lady</u> **in thy orisons be all my sins remembered.**

We could start our comparison of the two speeches by observing that Q1 shortens the traditional version. Including the **orisons** line (with which Hamlet addresses Ophelia), the Q1 version has 188 words, as against the traditional version's 276, and 23 lines vs. 35 lines. It is, in short, roughly 2/3 as long as the traditional version (68 per cent as many words, 65 per cent as many lines). Q1 greatly truncates the speech until **undiscover'd country** (for reasons we will examine) but then amplifies it. It remains suggestive of something foundational to the speech that the cue in each version is the same: **my sins remembered**.

Indeed, the Q1 soliloquy reproduces the beginning and end of the traditional version almost perfectly, and takes up many of its words and phrases intact. But only one line is wholly unchanged in the entire Q1 speech: **Than fly to others that we know not of**. The Q1 composer almost got the preceding line right, too, save for replacing

ills with <u>evils</u>. Of course, we can still hear **ills** within the latter word: <u>evils</u>, and this echo may help to explain the word that was eventually substituted. But a question about **Than fly to others that we know not of**: Why should this line, of all the lines that have since become famous from this speech, have been taken over without changes?

Perhaps because it is metrically regular, with eight simple, monosyllabic words. On the whole, the Q1 speech tends to have simpler vocabulary than its counterpart. Take the infamous <u>Ay, there's the point</u> for the traditional version's **that is the question**. This foregrounds something we see throughout Q1: its preference for easier words. Another instance comes with the traditional version's **bourn** (a noun, as in 'boundary'), which becomes <u>borne</u> (a verb, as in 'carried before') in <u>borne before an everlasting Judge</u>. Shakespeare's noun is the less usual of the two words, and, just as it prefers <u>point</u> to **question**, Q1 remembers the more common <u>borne</u> over **bourn**. Q1 also shows a preference for the kind of monosyllables we see in **Than fly to others that we know not of**. Of 19 polysyllabic words in the traditional version of the soliloquy, Q1 retained 8, or 42 per cent (a lower rate than the 68 per cent of its total words when compared with the traditional version). Q1 omits such words, for instance, as **contumely, devoutly, enterprises, insolence, natural, opposing, outrageous, question, resolution, traveller**, and **unworthy**. But we should note that while the composer of Q1 on the whole lacked Shakespeare's extensive vocabulary – or, at least, chose to keep the diction of his soliloquy simpler – he does substitute <u>passenger</u> for **traveller** and <u>flattery</u> for the traditional version's shorter **whips**.

One other phrase that remains largely intact is the suicide cue: **his ... quietus make, with a bare bodkin**. This is perhaps owing to the nature of the image. One of the most serious and frightening lines in the soliloquy, its reliance on the very unusual phrase **quietus make** probably contributed to its survival in Q1. This may be a case of a word and image being *so* unusual that the line is difficult to forget.

Likewise, Q1 keeps some of the traditional soliloquy's **and** pairings, such as **grunt and sweat**, and refashions a new one: <u>scorns and flattery</u>. But it drops many of the traditional version's reduplications, pairings like **slings and arrows, heart-ache and ... shocks, whips and scorns** (as an exact phrase), and **pitch and moment**. One could argue, of course, that these pairings are present in material that the Q1 composer chose not to reproduce (or was unable to recall), and are thus absent from Q1 merely because that material is absent. But surely this argument is circular (or, at least, potentially circular): it avoids the possibility that phrases such as **pitch and moment** are one of the reasons the Q1 composer either chose not to include the material or could not remember it in the first place. These phrases, again, seem 'redundant' in a poetic way. It is difficult not to feel that by themselves they come close to defining what poetry *is* by forcing us to examine the relation between similar-but-different words. Given only the traditional soliloquy, we could be tempted to say that its poetry lies in such phrases as **slings and arrows** and **pitch and moment**. Their absence in Q1 highlights its lesser interest in the imagination.

Q1 is shorter and simpler in its vocabulary, and it is also less dedicated to what we have earlier called 'thought.' Many of the traditional version's 'thought' words (words concerning the intellect, the imagination, and point of view) are missing in Q1. The latter keeps the words **conscience, dream**, and **know** – and even adds <u>sense</u> and two <u>hopes</u> (for **wish**) – but omits the words **mind, question, regard, resolution, respect**, and **thought.** In its substitution of <u>brain</u> for **mind**, in fact, we can see the larger tendency of Q1 to simplify the abstractions it encountered in the traditional soliloquy. A <u>brain</u> is a physical part of the body; **the mind** is a concept.

We observed that the traditional version of the soliloquy had a number of artful repetitions. Q1 has some repetitions as well, but they often four <u>Ay</u>s – its Hamlet talking to himself – versus only one in Shakespeare's version. A change in emphasis is this soliloquy's key word – <u>Ay</u> – versus the **no** of the traditional version. Perhaps this comes in part from Q1's abandoning (or forgetting) the traditional version's debate structure. Q1 does not have the traditional version's **whether** clause (this is one of its most extensive omissions, in fact). Nor does it have several of its defining clauses: **by a sleep to say, Thus, thus.** We could say that Q1's Ays, as well as its final O, stand in for these terms, just as the somewhat artless repetition of its Which ... which stands in for **Thus ... thus.** In each instance, Q1 replaces the stronger, coordinative terms of argument (**whether, thus**) with weaker, declarative alternatives: **Ay, which, O.**

The two speeches differ significantly in how they relate to hierarchy and power. The traditional version has a tacit acceptance of social hierarchy at its close. It follows its satirical complaints (**insolence of office**) with a deployment of heroic terms: **action, take arms, enterprises of great pitch and moment**, and so forth. Q1 omits most of these terms, and on the whole it seems more deferential to power of a religious nature. In its soliloquy, in fact, we wake up from death to face an everlasting Judge, and are divided into the happy and the accurs'd. This serves as a conventionally Christian portrait of the afterlife. As such, it comes in stark contrast to Hamlet's agnosticism in the traditional 'To be or not to be' speech. There, as we have seen, he insists that the only thing we can be sure of is our **dread.** It seems no accident that Q1 replaces **dread** with a hope of **something after death.** The word hope, in fact, is used twice, once as a joyful hope. Q1 also tells us that happy souls smile in the afterlife. This is perhaps not very surprising. Q1's scenarios of the sufferings of this life are simpler and melodramatic: the rich scorn us, the poor curse the rich, widows are oppressed, orphans wronged, and hunger obtains generally. Life is hard, but the afterlife will be a happy place for the happy. This confident religious sentiment jars (to say the least) with the suicide material that Q1 oddly retains from the traditional version.

One of the most revealing changes in the entire speech comes at its end, in a seemingly minor word. Q1 replaces Hamlet's **Nymph** with the term Lady. The two sentences finish the same way:

Nymph, in thy orisons be all my sins rememb'red.

> (traditional version)

Lady in thy orisons be all my sins rememb'red.

> (Q1 version)

The change is more than cosmetic. Or, if it is cosmetic, the choice of words tells us something more profound about the two soliloquies than one might guess. Hamlet has a number of options for addressing Ophelia. One of them is Q1's <u>Lady</u>, which in Shakespeare's time was a respectful term of address for a female aristocrat. It is much less 'marked' as a term than the traditional version's **Nymph**, which comes from the realm of pastoral poetry. It is the word that a young male courtier (such as Hamlet) could use flirtatiously in reference to a young, attractive female. Richard III uses this word sarcastically when he notes that he is not made for a lover's life. He complains that he is unable to '[caper] nimbly in a lady's chamber / To the lascivious pleasing of a lute,' or to 'strut before a wanton ambling nymph' (1.1.12–13, 17).

However Hamlet intends this word, when he addresses Ophelia as **Nymph** he calls up the scene that Richard mocks, and reminds us that he is a courtly aristocrat – in fact, a prince. If Q1 has decided that its 'To be or not to be' speech will be delivered by a more conventionally religious Hamlet, one not as concerned with thought and philosophy as the figure we get in the Q2 and Folio texts of *Hamlet*, it also works to downplay Hamlet's positive version of hierarchy – replacing it with a simpler, more conventionally Christian version of the afterlife. In Q1, the emphasis is not on the uncertainty of this life (and what it makes us endure here) but rather the certainty of the afterlife, where we get separated into the <u>happy</u> and the <u>accurs'd</u>. Some will be smiling, others not.

For Shakespeare's Hamlet, there is no reason for any of us to smile. This enormous change in the outlook of Q1 is matched by an equally important change to the Hamlet who utters it. In the traditional version of this speech, Hamlet is a skeptical aristocrat who, weighed down by his all-too-human **conscience**, speaks the language of a philosopher. In Q1, Hamlet has become a Baptist who counts himself among the <u>happy</u> who will <u>smile</u> for all eternity in **the undiscover'd country**. Although he speaks his speech more plainly, it is his different understanding of life, more than the changes in words between the two speeches, that makes the Q1 version much less mysterious than the 'To be or not to be' that Shakespeare wrote.

To be or not to be

To be, or not to be, that is the question:⁣ 55
Whether 'tis nobler in the mind to suffer
The slings and arrows of outrageous fortune,
Or to take arms against a sea of troubles,
And by opposing, end them. To die, to sleep –
No more, and by a sleep to say we end 60
The heart-ache and the thousand natural shocks
That flesh is heir to; 'tis a consummation
Devoutly to be wish'd. To die, to sleep –
To sleep, perchance to dream – ay, there's the rub,
For in that sleep of death what dreams may come, 65
When we have shuffled off this mortal coil,
Must give us pause; there's the respect
That makes calamity of so long life:
For who would bear the whips and scorns of time,
Th' oppressor's wrong, the proud man's contumely, 70
The pangs of despis'd love, the law's delay,
The insolence of office, and the spurns
That patient merit of th' unworthy takes,
When he himself might his quietus make
With a bare bodkin; who would fardels bear, 75
To grunt and sweat under a weary life,
But that the dread of something after death,
The undiscover'd country, from whose bourn
No traveller returns, puzzles the will,
And makes us rather bear those ills we have, 80
Than fly to others that we know not of?
Thus conscience does make cowards of us all,
And thus the native hue of resolution
Is sicklied o'er with the pale cast of thought,
And enterprises of great pitch and moment 85
With this regard their currents turn awry,
And lose the name of action. – Soft you now,
The fair Ophelia.

Consummation
(Some Conclusions)

This book began by imagining we could watch and listen to many thousands of performances of the 'To be or not to be' soliloquy down through history. As these images and sounds unfolded, we pictured ourselves taking note of the changing interpretations of the speech. The precedents that had once seemed to reassure performers later became problems, as actors strived to make their versions different from those that had come before. Four hundred years of performance history seemed to weigh on the most recent actors. Hamlet's own complaint about trudging wearily through life, weighed down by burdens, serves as a good description of the weight that many feel in relation to this soliloquy.

This is as true for readers as for actors. It is almost impossible today to avoid feeling the gravity of this speech, for the play's influence over four centuries has ensured it a primary place in our collective imagination. The 'To be or not to be' soliloquy, in fact, has become something like an unofficial metaphor for 'culture' in the West. Whatever else it is about, Hamlet's speech – residing at the heart of our most celebrated writer's most recognized play and character – is about culture itself.

This is one reason the most famous speech in the English language is also the most mysterious, and often poorly understood. Like many of our icons, we treat it with alternating reverence and satire.

Thus it is at one and the same time solidly monumental, like an enormous marble statue, and humorously overinflated, like a helium balloon regularly punctured in the popular media. Taken at these extremes, 'To be or not to be' can remain as elusive as the character who speaks it.

As we have seen, though, there are other reasons for the speech's difficulty. We compared its repetitions and recursions to several things: to an internalization of the dueling angels of the morality play tradition; to a snake's winding coils; to the challenge of hopping from stone to stone in the midst of a moving stream; to watching a tennis match that moves unpredictably from court to court while a point is in progress. In its chilling philosophy, we saw, the speech worked as a rhetorical version of Medusa's petrifying gaze. So complicated and intricate is the 'To be or not to be' soliloquy that each of these analogies seems incomplete without the others. We called it a 'messy' speech, but its messiness is not only disorder. It is a disorder that hypnotizes – even freezes – us with unpredictable rhythms and patterns.

We all struggle with the speech in part because its speaker struggles as he delivers it. Actors tend to dislike this speech not only because of the weight of precedence it carries with it, but also because its complicated rhythms and directions are notoriously difficult to master. As we have seen, Shakespeare puts something like the whole of *Hamlet* within its lines; this abundance of material means that delivering the soliloquy is tantamount to performing a play within the play. This complex compression is another reason the most famous speech in literature is so poorly understood: like the play of which it is a part, the soliloquy has an epic reach and scope.

This quality makes the 'To be or not to be' soliloquy difficult to see clearly. We noted that the 'suicide' interpretation had become a shortcut for many readers. The awful truth the soliloquy advances is different. Hamlet's regret over the role that thinking takes in our life offers a more painful insight into the human condition.

Hamlet's inward guest works as a kind of grinning skull that mocks human achievement and ability. Far from a hymn to self-consciousness, Hamlet's soliloquy expresses profound misgivings about the process of thinking 'too much.' If the 'suicide' interpretation is an error in one direction, the 'Hamlet as philosopher' reading makes a mistake the other way.

A difficult question we asked at the outset of this book has gone unaddressed until now. What does it mean that the central speech of the central character in the central play of the language's central author is all but useless to its speaker and story? Unlike some of his other soliloquies, 'To be or not to be' does little if anything for Hamlet or his play. He enters, speaks, and breaks off when Ophelia walks in view, and what he has said concerning dread and death produces few if any reverberations in the world of the play. It is, instead, a kind of set piece or jewel, a rhythmical grumble that has survived in our culture even as it indicts the pettiness of survival. In its attainment of status, gaining a reputation as a speech of great pitch and moment, 'To be or not to be' has ironically done something that Hamlet says we cannot do.

We should end this book, then, with the speech's own relation to books. Surely it means something that, in the Q1 version of *Hamlet*, both Ophelia and Hamlet are described as holding books in their hands as this speech unfolds. This may be a recognition, by the actors who remembered Shakespeare's play, not only of the reading that Hamlet does elsewhere, but also of the speech's essentially literary nature. The soliloquy's triumph as a cultural document may depend, as literature itself does, on the fact that it makes nothing happen. It is necessary to neither Hamlet nor *Hamlet*. And it is not necessary to them in precisely the way that literature is not necessary to life. One secret of the 'To be or not to be' soliloquy is that it has survived as a symbol of so much of our culture – literature, the theater, and philosophy – by doing no more and no less than what these cultural forms and activities themselves do. Play and character do not need the soliloquy, but neither would they be imaginable without it. By putting so much of a life and a play within the speech, Shakespeare has ensured that – like play and character – it is both difficult and durable.

Acknowledgments and Further Reading

Soliloquies can seem fairly isolated things, but no one who reads or writes on Shakespeare's works – least of all *Hamlet* – does so in isolation. There is quite simply no end of scholarly comment on this great work, so it is only proper here that I register my great debts to a host of scholars and critics who have published on this soliloquy. I should start by admitting that my favorite edition of any Shakespeare play is Harold Jenkins's *Hamlet* for the 2nd New Arden series (originally published in 1982). Readers will sense my continual reliance here upon his judicious scholarship and commentary. One of the most stimulating re-interpretations of Hamlet and *Hamlet* in recent years is that of my colleague Eric Mallin in *Inscribing the Time: Shakespeare and the End of Elizabethan England* (1995); readers will notice that I have borrowed the idea of an infectious Hamlet from Mallin's book. I have also benefitted from Mary Z. Maher's fine *Modern Hamlets and Their Soliloquies* (1992), as well as from notes and articles by such critics as, among others, Henry Chadwick, James E. Hirsh, E. A. J. Honigmann, Alex Newell, Vincent F. Petronella, Irving T. Richards, and Gary Taylor. Those interested in pursuing these essays will be able to trace them through the World Shakespeare Database, an invaluable online resource for research into Shakespeare's life and works. On Shakespeare's soliloquies generally, readers may consult Wolfgang Clemens's *Shakespeare's Soliloquies*

(1964). For the soliloquies in *Hamlet*, see Alex Newell, *The Soliloquies in Hamlet: The Structural Design* (1991). Roland Frye's *The Renaissance 'Hamlet': Issues and Responses in 1600* (1984) and the journal *Hamlet Studies* (1979–) are extremely useful as well. Those interested in the strange little book called Q1 are urged to consult a foundational collection of essays edited by Thomas Clayton: *The 'Hamlet' First Published (Q1, 1603): Origins, Form, Intertextualities* (1992). In the preparation of this book, I have been greatly aided by my student and research assistant, Jennifer Dixon. It was Dixon who first taught me the peculiar value of the speech in Q1; in addition, the insight as to *Hamlet*'s presence in the soliloquy is fully hers. Along with Dixon, my colleagues Martin Kevorkian, Eric Mallin, and Elizabeth Scala read this book in draft and offered characteristically generous and insightful suggestions. I am glad to be able to express my debts to them here.

Index

A Note to the Reader:

This index has two sections. The first section lists major subjects and themes related to the 'To be or not to be' soliloquy itself. The second gives the names of real persons, characters from 'Hamlet', and other proper nouns mentioned in the text. For ease of reference, the full text of Hamlet's 'To be or not to be' soliloquy is printed before each chapter of this book on pages x, 6, 12, 42, 64, 86, 100, and is paired with the less familiar Q1 version on pages 91–3. Discussion of the meanings of particular words and phrases in the speech takes place throughout the book, but is especially concentrated in chapter 3 ('There's the Rub'), pages 13–41.

'To be or not to be': The Speech

People, Characters, Plays, and Things